AF544718

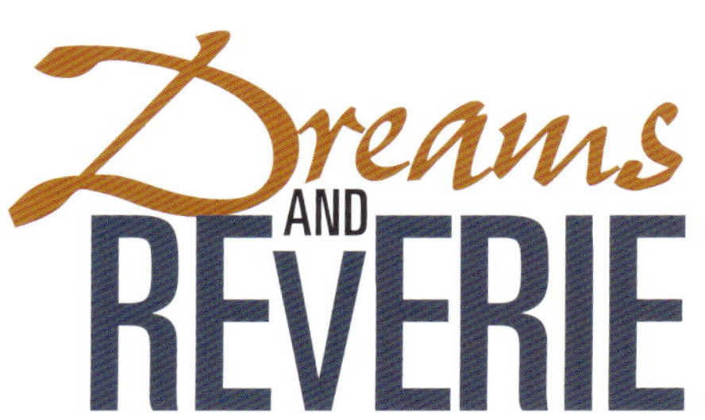
Dreams
AND
REVERIE

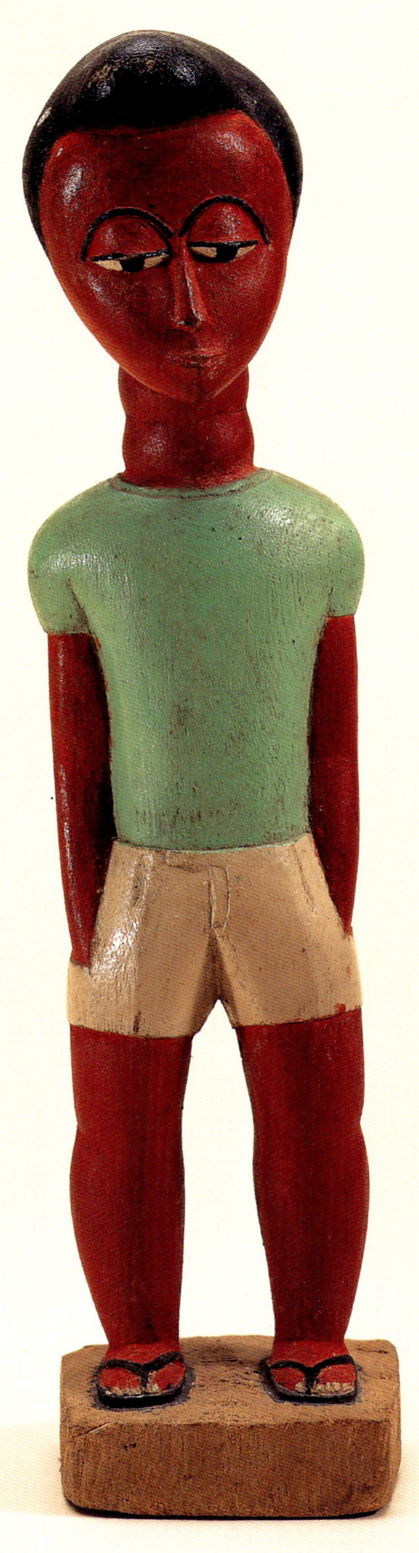

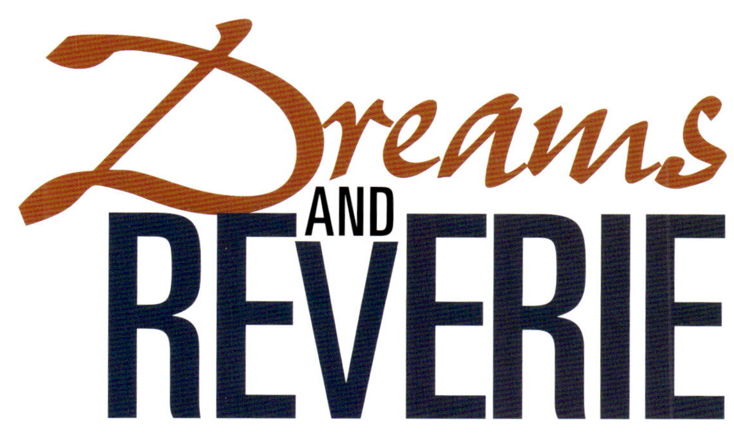

IMAGES OF OTHERWORLD MATES AMONG THE BAULE, WEST AFRICA

PHILIP L. RAVENHILL

SMITHSONIAN INSTITUTION PRESS
Washington and London

ACQUIRING EDITOR: Amy Pastan
COPY EDITOR: Catherine F. McKenzie
PRODUCTION EDITOR: Jack Kirshbaum
DESIGNER: Janice Wheeler
PRODUCTION MANAGER: Ken Sabol

Library of Congress Cataloging-in-Publication Data

Ravenhill, Philip L.
Dreams and reverie : Images of otherworld mates among the Baule, West Africa / Philip L. Ravenhill
p. cm.
ISBN 1-56098-650-6 (cloth : alk. paper)
1. Sculpture, Baule. 2. Wood-carving, Baule. 3. Sculpture, African—Côte d'Ivoire. 4. Sexuality in art. 5. Man-woman relationships--Côte d'Ivoire. I. Title
NB1255.C85R38 1996
730'.89'963385—dc20 95-48291

British Library Cataloging-in-Publication data available

Manufactured in Hong Kong
00 99 98 97 96 5 4 3 2 1

∞ The paper used in this publication meets the minimum requirements of the American National Standard for Permanence of Paper for Printed Library Materials Z39.48-1984.

Frontispiece: Figure of an otherworld man with barbershop hair style, neck lines, shirt, shorts, and sandals, c. 1965, height 27 cm. Fowler Museum of Cultural History, UCLA. X94.77.13.

Photographic credits: Franko Khoury (1, 4, 6, 8, 26); Denis Nervig (ii, 2, 3, 5, 7, 9, 10, 16–23, 25, 27); Lap Nguyen Tien (11, 12, 14, 15); Philip Ravenhill (13, 24).

Il faut se contenter de découvrir,

mais se garder d'expliquer.

—Georges Braque

One must be content with discovering,

and refrain from explaining.

CONTENTS

PREFACE

This book is the result of an ongoing consideration of the meaning of Baule (pronounced bough-lay) figurative art produced in the postcolonial age. The search for meaning has not ended, nor has the topic of research been exhausted. Indeed I have come to think of my enterprise not so much as research in art history but as a reflexive quest, a quest for sympathetic discovery of what art can be—can do—in the life of an individual.

In 1972 I went to Côte d'Ivoire to undertake research for my Ph.D. in social anthropology,[1] and at that time I had little interest in art except perhaps as a reflection of social organization, as something illustrative of other realities. During two years of residence in the villages of Agbao and Kounaïri, however, I discovered art as it was experienced in the public performances of masked personae who intervened in village life when men died or, subsequently, when their deaths were formally remembered in public ceremony. In observing the solitary dance of the Goli mask (which makes it possible for a man's body to be interred) and the choreographed sorties of the entire pantheon of Goli masks (which months later make possible his "second funeral" and the renewal of normal life), I began to get a glimmer at least of the importance of art in the lives of the people with whom I lived.[2] After finishing my dissertation, I returned to Côte d'Ivoire to continue my investigations into the Goli masquerade. It was then, while I was living in the town of Bouaké, that a door into another world of art—Baule figurative art—was fortuitously opened for me. In the reality and immediacy of lived experience, rather than in the artificial exchanges of researcher and informants, I gradually learned about how, for the Baule, an otherworld known as the *blolo* (pronounced blaw-law) impinged on human existence.

I was already familiar with carved Baule figures (especially those produced in the period after World War II) that were offered for sale by local *antiquaires* to foreigners. I also had a general understanding of the cultural genre of figures that represented otherworld men and women, *blolo bian* (otherworld man) and *blolo bla* (otherworld woman). Yet I had little real understanding of what place the *blolo*, the otherworld, actually occupied in the thought and experience of Baule individuals. Over a period of months that stretched into years, I experienced vicariously the *blolo* and its denizens through discussions with a friend, Albert Koffi Kouadio, during the critical and transitional period of his life of courtship and marriage to his girlfriend Jacqueline.[3]

The basic approach that I have used as an anthropologist studying art and aesthetics is exegetical: I examine the intentional aspects of the art, and I seek to elucidate the conceptual framework from which the art derives its meaning. Thus I rely heavily on the analysis of indigenous terms, and while I excuse myself in advance should this make the reader's task more difficult, I would nonetheless stress the absolute necessity of this method if contextual studies of art are to advance. The initial examination of a traditional art form must be devoted to the ideas of its creators, users, and viewers. It is only when this essential task is complete that one can develop other, more universal or pancultural theories and aesthetics. Otherwise one sees in art something other than its creators intended.

I do not argue for art as a reflection of culture, since art is more often dynamic than static and creates culture just as much as it is created by culture. My initial exploration of Baule figurative art looks at it within various culturally determined processes: the productive process of its commissioning and consecration; the subsequent, interactive process between the user, the art, and the spirit represented; and the ongoing and complex process of male-female dialogue within which the art finds a place.

Over the past fifteen years my examinations of this genre of Baule art have led me to a personal reconsideration of the anthropological paradigm that has so influenced African art studies. In restricting investigation to cultural canons, the anthropological model has all too often been limited to normative descriptions of *typical works of art*, an oxymoron. I would argue that the power of any work of art lies in its concrete specificity, even though its creation occurs necessarily within the context of a preexisting, socially constructed reality.

This book is thus a personal statement about my own experience of the ultimate inadequacy of approaches to African art that reduce it to conventionality, predictability, mere functionality, or ahistorical epiphenomenon. It is a plea for the investigation of the specificity and power of *individual* objects in their original context. It is also a plea for an approach that is not limited to a description of artistic genres and aesthetic canons at the level of culture and society (i.e., in terms of the *tribe*, although that word by now is most often studiously avoided) but that, instead, investigates the specific arenas in which actual works of art are created, perceived, used, and appreciated, in the fullest sense of that word, by individual people and groups. Rather than explanation, my goal is understanding.

My first attempt to present an exegesis of Baule thought about otherworld figures was my 1980 publication *Baule Statuary Art: Meaning and Modernization*.

That essay, whose two parts have been revised as Chapters One and Two of this volume, serves as a convenient point of entry to Baule figurative art, a personal baseline for my subsequent ruminations. In these two chapters I examine the culturally constructed meaning inherent in Baule figurative art, and I seek to demonstrate that the modernization of this art by the incorporation of Western elements of dress is a logical application of the Baule idea that the sculpted figurative form be judged by the same aesthetic criteria as human form.

Chapter Three received its initial impetus from a last-minute invitation in 1989 by Suzanne Blier to participate in the panel "Psychology and Art" for the annual meeting of the African Studies Association. My paper, "The Self and the Other: Physical Representations of Nonphysical Beings in Baule Statuary Art," grappled with ideas that had lain dormant for years.[4] Once articulated, the subject kept gnawing at me, and gradually my explorations expanded into Chapters Three and Four. They seek to move beyond a simple recourse to the explanation afforded by the cultural canon and to ask questions as to how *blolo* figures might have been of influence—and what these objects might have meant—in the individual existences of their original owners. Art perdures, and interpretations of it are always approximations. Thankfully one can return to the object to experience it anew and to attempt to formulate new reasons for its evocative power. These interpretations are but my current thoughts.

In 1990 Herbert Cole invited me to deliver a paper for the conference "Deceptive Realities: Authenticity and Quality in African Art" at the University of California at Santa Barbara. That paper has grown into Chapter Five, "Outside Imaginings: The Object as Souvenir," in which I consider the reasons for the initial misinterpretation of modern Baule figures and the subsequent creation of a new replica genre.

The book closes with the *envoi* of Chapter Six, "Vehicles of Reverie," musings on the other worlds that are created by art. Not in any way a conclusion, it simply acknowledges that the quest for meaning, understanding, and appreciation continue.

The influence and help of others have greatly enhanced my work on this volume. Chapters Three through Six owe their existence to different external stimuli and to an ongoing, personal intrigue with the wonder of the otherworld as experienced by the Baule. The Baule concept of the otherworld has been for me an enigma, always present in its general form but perceived from new angles and points of view as I have reflected upon it afresh, typically while reading or rereading books that have been particularly provocative in raising ideas about human experience and the meaning of art. While rereading Gaston Bachelard's *The Poetics of Reverie*, I suddenly saw how the notion of daytime reverie complemented my appreciation of Baule ideas about the dreamed otherworld; his thoughts inspired my ideas for this book and its title. David Freedberg's *The Power of Images* has been another seminal influence. Although he deals largely with Western art history, Freedberg raises a host of issues concerning images and responses to them that have an immediate resonance to Baule experience. Susan Stewart's brilliant book, *On Longing,* has been another significant influence, especially on my thoughts concerning the object as souvenir (Chapter Five). Finally, as I was beginning to write the final chapter, I read anew *The Life of Forms in Art* by Henri Focillon, whose ideas influenced my final reflections. I use the thoughts of these and other authors throughout the book as intellectual foils that, held against my interpretations of Baule experience and art, have revealed new facets of understanding or provoked new imaginings. This book is very much about imagining—about trying empathetically to imagine how the belief in an otherworld mate might influence one's very being. My own imaginings commingle with Baule imaginings about that distant, other place.

This book owes much to conversations and exchanges with many colleagues and friends over many years. I owe a major debt to my mentor, Tom Beidelman, who introduced me to both anthropology and the writings of Gaston Bachelard—especially *The Poetics of Reverie* and *The Poetics of Space*—and who has always provided intellectual stimulation through his never flagging quest to understand the human condition and to translate culture. At different stages of writing, a number of colleagues have read drafts of various chapters and offered me their opinions. I am grateful to Herbert Cole for his encouragement over the years and for his ongoing commitment to African art of the twentieth century. Rachel Hoffman has been a constant and stimulating interlocutor, reading several chapters, offering wise comments, and above all urging me onward. Doran Ross has been a steady friend for many years and has consistently cheered me on, finding fascination in the topics of my inquiry and making it possible for me to explore Baule figurative art in the exhibition *Spirits as People: Figurative Art of the Baule, Côte d'Ivoire* that we co-organized at the UCLA Fowler Museum of Cultural History in 1994. To him and the entire staff of the museum I owe a special thanks. Irena Averkieff, who edited my monograph *The Self and the Other* for that exhibition, also kindly gave the present manuscript a first reading.

Sylvia Williams, Director of the National Museum of African Art from 1983 until her untimely death in February 1996, was a wonderful colleague and friend who consistently encouraged my writing. She also endorsed my application for support from the Regents' Publication Fund of the Smithsonian Institution, which permitted me a two-month sabbatical to revise existing chapters and to write the final two chapters. I would like to acknowledge my personal debt to Sylvia for nine years of challenging and fruitful collaboration.

During my sabbatical, Dr. Roslyn Walker assumed charge of the Curatorial

Department and made it possible for me to write without interruption. To her and other fellow curators—Bryna Freyer, Andrea Nicolls, and Lydia Puccinelli—my most profound thanks for sharing the burden. Toni Evans, administrative assistant in the department, has always cheerfully supported my work and made life more easy and pleasant than it otherwise might have been.

The photographs in this book result from the skills of three excellent photographers. Lap Nguyen Tien worked with me in Côte d'Ivoire and produced stunning images of art *in situ*. Denis Nervig photographed the figures in the collection of the Fowler Museum, and Franko Khoury photographed the ones in the National Museum of African Art. All three have applied their artistry to Baule figurative art and facilitated its appreciation.

Research in Côte d'Ivoire was undertaken while I was on a postdoctoral grant from the Wenner-Gren Foundation for Anthropological Research and also while I was employed by the Institut d'Histoire, d'Art et d'Archéologie africains of the Université Nationale in Abidjan. The support of both institutions, which made possible the research for this book, is gratefully acknowledged. Dr. Victor Diabaté, former Director of the Institut d'Histoire, d'Art et d'Archéologie africains, was a faithful supporter of my research. Dr. Susan Vogel read closely my first publication on Baule figurative art, and her groundbreaking research on Baule aesthetics has stimulated my own. I am thankful to Dr. Judith Timyan for her help in the interpretation of Baule terms and their proper transcription. Yaya Savané of the Musée National in Abidjan has shared my enthusiasm for the modern period of African art and has been a long-time partner in dialogue. To El Hadji Baba Ilori, whose eye educated mine over many years, I offer images for his commentary and for a shared nostalgia of a special period of time some twenty years ago.

Finally, there are three special beings: Geoffrey, Brendan, and Amanda. They have brought untold joy to my life. They have tolerated my retreats for writing, and they have been, and are, constant reminders of other realities. This book is for them.

A NOTE ON TRANSCRIPTION

My transcription of Baule terms does not take into account certain phonetic differences: *o* is used to transcribe both the sounds of closed and open *o* vowels, and similarly *e* is used to transcribe the different sounds of closed and open *e* vowels. The vowel sounds in the word *blolo* are open vowels, and the word is pronounced "blaw'law." Nasalized vowels are written as a vowel followed by *n*.

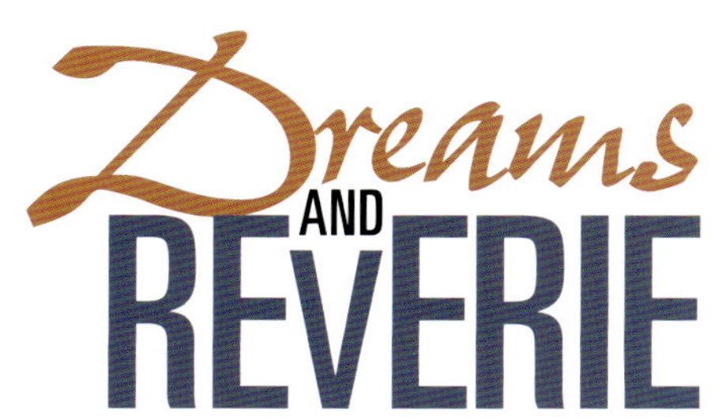
Dreams
AND
REVERIE

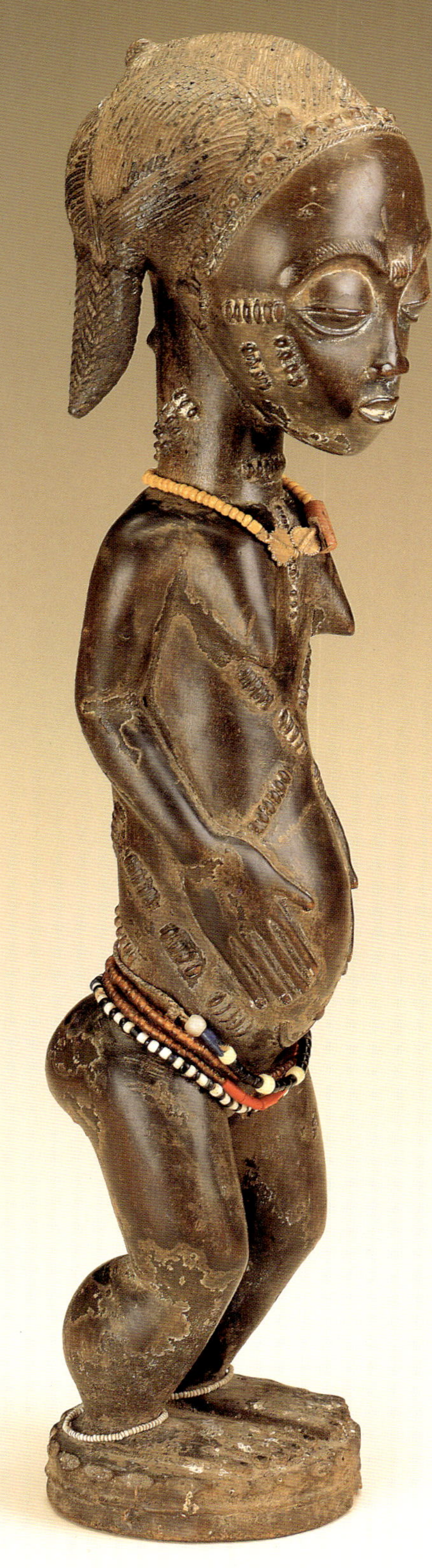

Chapter One

THE MEANING OF BAULE STATUES

Although in the literature on African art, Baule statues have often been referred to as ancestor figures, Susan Vogel (1973, 1978) has pointed out that these wooden people (*waka sran*) are in fact carved to represent either nature spirits (*asie usu*) or otherworld men or otherworld women (*blolo bian* and *blolo bla,* respectively).[1] While nature spirits are of various types having varying roles, they have in common the inducement of abnormal effects upon the people with whom they establish contact. The effect may be detrimental or beneficial, bringing about, for example, mental troubles, increased luck in hunting, or the power of clairvoyance, and the contact can be either controlled or maintained by sacrificial offerings. The form of statues representing the nature spirits known as *bo usu* (forest spirits) may be minimal, demonstrating a general human form but without detail, for like the spirits that they represent they are dwarflike (*angbe*).[2] Statues representing these spirits often become encrusted with blood, for they can be considered to be fetishes (*amuin*)[3] and it is "with blood that fetishes become powerful" (*mmoja ye man amuin o yo nna*). In contradistinction to the statues of these nature spirits, which often require a plural form, are the individual statues that are carved to represent a man's otherworld woman or a woman's otherworld man. It is to these carefully looked after statues representing otherworld people that this book is devoted.

1. Figure of an otherworld woman wearing a beaded necklace with gold jewels, hip beads, and anklet beads, c. 1900, height 48.9 cm. National Museum of African Art, museum purchase, 85-15-2.

THE *BLOLO*, OR OTHERWORLD

In Baule thought the *blolo,* or otherworld, exists in contrast to the world of physical reality. Etymologically, *blolo* is derived from *blo,* meaning "to claim, to praise, to vaunt," and *lo* is a locational noun that can be glossed as "there."[4] Thus the sense of the word is "the place that is vaunted," with the implicit idea that although it is a place that is spoken well of, in fact, no concrete confirmation of its desirable attributes has ever been found. The locational component of *blolo—lo,* or "there"—makes explicit the contrast with life "on the earth *here*" (*asie'n su wa*). The *blolo* is a world that exists parallel to the lived world experienced by men and women, and is considered to be the world of the dead. Yet the *blolo* is far more than the abode of the departed dead, for it is also the place of origin for the spirits of the newborn. Thus a newborn is seen as originating from his otherworld mother (*blolo nin*),[5] and his meconium, or first bowel movement, is referred to as otherworld feces (*blolo bi*). In the event of an untimely early death, an explanation is provided by saying "his otherworld mother took him back" (*i blolo nin yeo fe lo*). It is also in this otherworld (*blolo*) that each person "on this earth here" (*asie'n su wa*) has a person of the opposite sex to whom he or she is inexorably linked: the otherworld woman (*blolo bla*) or the otherworld man (*blolo bian*).

OTHERWORLD MATES

Initial knowledge of one's otherworld man or woman usually proceeds from a particular crisis of young adult life, such as sterility, and as Vogel (1973:25) points out, these crises are almost always of a sexual nature. In consultation with a diviner (*wunnzueyifue*), one may find that the problem results from the unhappiness or jealousy of one's neglected otherworld sexual opposite. In such a case, divination may reveal that it is necessary to represent this otherworld person by a statue carved in human form to which offerings of food or money can be made on a regular basis and that it is also necessary to consecrate one night of the week to this *blolo* person by sleeping alone.[6] Additional knowledge of one's otherworld sexual partner is gained by the dreams (*lalie*) that one has on nights set aside for him or her. Two important points must be made in relation to these dreams: (l) there is an implicit encouragement of such dreams as well as an expectation that they will be sexual in nature; and (2) this anticipation of regular nocturnal dream visits by an otherworld lover inevitably leads to a certain continuity in the contents of such dreams—a continuity that maintains an ongoing interpersonal relationship.

In dream visits one's otherworld mate does not necessarily assume a fixed form, being able to take on the form of any person of the opposite sex, whether real or imaginary, with the exception of one's spouse. Thus in the concept of an otherworld lover, there is an implicit contrast of one's actual spouse to all other possible sexual (not marital) partners. There are various English glosses for the translations of the terms *blolo bian* and *blolo bla,* but I have studiously refrained from translating these terms as "otherworld husband" or "otherworld wife." This is because the use of *bian* and *bla* is significant in indicating that the relation is not with a husband (*wun*) or wife (*yi*), culturally defined *social* relations. While the term *bian* may be used in the context of matrimonial relations (Carteron 1972)—in contrast to the term *yasua* (also glossed as "male"), which is only used as a component of kinship terms designating "people with whom it is inconceivable that a female Ego can entertain sexual relations" (Étienne 1972:66–67)—I would argue that its inherent emphasis is on sexual availability and thus that it stands in contrast to the word for husband, which suggests a legally recognized social relationship. The word *bla,* glossed as "woman" or "female," marks "simultaneously the sexual characteristic and the social dimension including marital, and corresponds to the two masculine terms *yasua* and *bian*" (Carteron 1972). I would thus reaffirm my argument for the essentially sexual nature of the relation with one's *blolo bian* or *blolo bla,* which stands in marked contrast to the polyvalent relation to a real-world spouse. The sexual connotation inherent in both *bian* and *bla* is confirmed in the Baule words for those who commit adultery: *bladifwe* (adulterer, or woman-sleeper) and *biandifwe* (adulteress, or man-sleeper) (Effimbra 1959:112).

The relationship with one's otherworld man or woman must also be seen as a relationship with an isolated individual and not a relationship with a social actor embedded in a nexus of relationships with various social groups. Thus, for example, although one's otherworld mate is an individual with a specific name (usually revealed in divination), it is significant that the name is limited to a personal name without a patronymic (*si dunman*). A *blolo bla,* for instance, may have the name Akisi (given to a girl born on Monday) but would never have the name Kuaku Akisi, or Akisi the daughter of Kuaku. Similarly it would appear that a *blolo bla* or *-bian* never has a name such as Big Kuadyo (Kuadyo Dan) or Little Amlan (Amlan Kan), since such names result from the need to differentiate their bearers with other same-named kin.

If the relationship between a man and his otherworld woman or between a woman and her otherworld man is a dyadic sexual relationship between individuals, this is not to say that the relationship is without effect on relationships in the real world. As might be expected, the acknowledged existence of the otherworld mate is of particular importance to one's real-world spouse. The relations between a man and the *blolo bian* of his wife and between a woman and the *blolo bla* of her husband are characterized by a basic jealousy or rivalry (*wla*). In Baule kinship terminology, co-wives refer to each other as "rival" (*wla*), as do two men who are fundamentally linked by being married to sisters. In the same way, one's spouse and one's otherworld lover are considered to be rivals competing for the attentions of the person through whom they are linked. This relationship, however, is not a relationship between *equals;* a basic dissymmetry exists, since the otherworld paramour necessarily precedes the real-world spouse chronologically. Thus a man's *blolo bla* is considered his first woman (*bla kpenngben*) with the rights and privileges (especially permanence) which accrue to that position, and his actual spouse can be seen as being in the relatively inferior position of his later woman (*bla sien*).

Jealousy, however, is not incompatible with a relatively higher social position, and the *blolo bla,* for example, may prove to be particularly pestering or mischief making because of her envy of a man's real-world sexual partner, whether wife or not. A young man told me that once when sleeping with a young woman on the night supposedly reserved for his *blolo bla* he was awakened by the insistent tugs of his sexual partner, who said she had just dreamed of his otherworld woman, who fought with her to chase her from his side. Dreaming of the otherworld lover of one's spouse appears to be a relatively common experience. Another young man reported that he frequently dreams of fighting with his fiancée's *blolo bian,* who is a veteran of the French army, an *ancien combattant* (see chap. 2), and thus, significantly, older than he. Furthermore, the perception of competition between a person and his or her spouse's otherworld sexual partner is reinforced when he or she experiences the rivalry not only in reported activities but also in participatory dreams.

DIFFERENCES BETWEEN OTHERWORLD MEN AND WOMEN

Although the difference between the notions of *blolo bla* and *blolo bian* would at first glance appear to be mainly a matter of gender, as indicated lexically, a fundamental dissymmetry of ideas exists concerning the respective attributes and characters of otherworld men and otherworld women. Pierre Étienne, the foremost recent student of the Baule, has stated that

> the *blolo bla* is much less worrisome than the *blolo bian.* It is above all he who renders a wife sterile, makes her give birth to still-born babies, or causes her children to die at an early age, and it is necessary to appease his jealousy regarding the terrestrial husband. We thus have a classic case of the inversion of relations between the here-below (*ici-bas*) and the here-after (*au-delà*). Here below it is, above all, women who are jealous among themselves; but in the hereafter this sexual jealousy is projected onto the relations between men. (1974:219 n. 33; my translation)[7]

This imbalance of attributes, the *blolo bian* being inherently more bothersome and jealous than the *blolo bla,* is reflected in a numerical disproportion between male and female statues. From four years' observation of the art market in the town of Bouaké in the early 1970s, I believe that male statues outnumber female statues by a ratio of at least five to one.[8]

How can one explain the difference between male and female otherworld mates and the fact that male mates are more often represented by statues than female mates? Otherworld men or women receive formal representation in wood only after it has been found that they are the cause of problems afflicting their partners in the real world. The higher likelihood of a woman requiring a statue for her spirit mate is perhaps because, for her, a problem with sterility is inescapable, whereas a man's sterility may not be publicly apparent thanks to his wife's independent solution. The common attitude of the

Baule is that sterility affects women more often than men, and if one of the more common reasons for having an otherworld man carved is sterility (see Vogel 1973:25, 1978:159), this may partially explain the higher incidence of male figures.

Further insight into the more problematic character of otherworld men as opposed to otherworld women can be gained from an examination of the polygynous nature of Baule society.[9] With polygyny there is a profound difference between the legitimated status of a man linked to two (or more) women and the nonlicit status of a woman linked to two men. From the Baule point of view, the man is seen as having an additional partner whereas the woman is seen as having an alternate partner. Should a Baule man decide to acquire an additional wife, certain social rules (concerning, for example, the equality of rights for co-wives) must be respected. If he abides by the normal social conventions, the second marriage is not unduly difficult. However, as a popular saying goes, "Since the Eternal One created day, no one has ever said that a woman could marry two men!" (*ke Anannganman a bo alie'n, be se'a ke bla ja bian nnyon*).[10] Étienne has only half-facetiously stated that "a prudent Baule man without being polygynous has available in different degrees three women: one with whom he is parting company, a second with whom he is fully married, and a third whom he is trying to marry" (1972:20; my translation). So-called serial monogamy, however, is of a different order for men and women; for a man, the chronological overlap of partners is socially condoned, but for a woman, it is socially prohibited.

As in the case of a real-world first woman, the pardon (*yaci*) of a man's otherworld first woman (*bla kpenngben*) must be demanded before a later woman (*bla sien*) is taken to wife.[11] For a man the asking of pardon is a rather informal matter that does not require public ceremony, perhaps because his having simultaneous sexual partners does not pose a problem. But for a woman the transition from an unmarried to a married state is often effected by a formal public ceremony that has as its goal the transferal of rights from an otherworld sexual partner to a real-world husband. This ceremony is called *atonvle,* a term that can be etymologized as *a-to-nvle,* or "the fall of change," and whose basic meaning appears to be approximately equivalent to "changeover."[12]

Atonvle ceremonies are also performed for a number of other purposes, depending in part, it appears, upon cultural practices in different Baule regions. Carteron (1972) and Guerry (1972:40) indicate that a ceremony may be conducted as a *rite de passage* for a girl at her menarche; Mona and Pierre Étienne (1964:153; 1971:172f) and Timothy Weiskel (1980:23–24) discuss a type of marriage called *atonvle,* in which rights to a woman are definitively transferred from a woman's family to that of her husband. My own research indicates that these ceremonies may be performed for first pregnancies, for the ending of mourning for a widow or widower, and even to reintegrate or cleanse a person who has fallen into a deep latrine of the sort usually dug in the bush near cultivated fields. Each of these ceremonies can be seen as a transitional rite in which normal time is suspended in order to effect a change in status (see Leach 1961). The formality of the occasion is marked by the special dress of the participants, a woman being dressed in finery with obligatory gold jewelry, and a man wearing a formal dress robe.

The special ceremony undertaken to change the relation between a woman and her otherworld man (*blolo bian*) takes place on the day after a night reserved for his dream visits. Having thus refrained from sexual relations, she is not "used" (*nvuen*) as she would have been had she just slept with a man, and she is thus ready to approach formally her *blolo bian*. The woman for whom the ceremony is performed, the *atonvle bla (atonvle* woman), cooks a cock, provided by her future husband, and a hen, provided by herself, and with these offerings she formally asks the pardon (*yaci*) of her otherworld man so that she may enter into a permanent relation with a real-world spouse. The food, although offered to the *blolo bian,* is actually eaten by the *atonvle bla* and the *atonvle yasua* (*atonvle* male),[13] who is a young man chosen to be a stand-in (*ijanunfue*) for the *blolo bian.* The *atonvle bla* and the *atonvle yasua,* both formally attired, spend the time from midmorning to midafternoon (or later) enclosed alone in a house where they eat the sacrificial meal and sleep. Thus, one of the main components of the ceremony is a period of suspension that ruptures the normal flow of time and serves as a line of demarcation between before-and-after periods of time.

DIVINATION, DEPICTION, AND CONSECRATION

Each Baule figure that represents, and thus appeases, an otherworld mate results from two processes: divination and sculpture. In Baule divination, conclusions are reached from an extended dialogue between the diviner, the client, his or her spouse, and attendant families. This dialogue is directed by the diviner's speech as he reads his divinatory instrument (the symbol-laden laces of *ngoinman* or the beaded sticks jumbled together by the mouse oracle)[14] and confirms or denies the various propositions put forth by one or the other party. The role of the diviner is to probe, the role of the client is to talk freely, and the role of the divining tool is to channel the flow of discourse. Conclusions are not fiats put forth by the diviner but flow directly from the recounted past and the present situation of the client.

In a case in which the problem under discussion is ultimately interpreted to be a result of the influence of one's otherworld mate, divination may also reveal that the problem can be resolved by the carving of a statuary stand-in that can receive conciliatory offerings. Then it becomes necessary to initiate the carving process—and I use the term "carving process" advisedly, for it is held that a carver should not rush a carving but should allow time for the otherworld mate to manifest his or her desires concerning the manner of physical representation. The artist who carves the statue acquires information concerning the otherworld person's physical form in different ways: it may result from the client-diviner dialogue or from the client's dreams of the spirit mate, or the otherworld person may even reveal himself or herself directly to the carver in dream visits. Whatever the source of the information, the goal of the carving is to depict the otherworld mate in a way that will please him or her.

Once the artist finishes and releases the carving, the client holds a lodging (*sike*) ceremony to consecrate it. The client formally addresses the otherworld mate, informing the mate that he or she now has a statuary stand-in that will henceforth receive small offerings of food or money on his or her behalf. In time the surface of the statue may be modified by the handling and the attention it receives during offerings; it may also be cleaned, rubbed with oil, wiped with kaolin, redyed, or painted. As the relationship between a person and his or her otherworld mate develops, the spirit partner may even ask for a new statuary representation to replace one with which he or she has become dissatisfied. Given that the otherworld both mirrors the real world and exists parallel to it, it is not surprising that Baule cultural canons of human beauty largely influence the aesthetic considerations that govern the carving of these statues.

BAULE AESTHETICS

In the Baule aesthetic[15] of both human and statuary form, the principal criterion is one of the golden mean; a given physical attribute should ideally be just so (*sese*), being neither too pronounced nor too diminutive. However, the exact combination of characteristics that result in the perfect form differ from culture to culture. When the Baule say that a neck should not be too long ("like a camel's") or too short ("like a cricket's") or too thick, they do not mean thereby that a neck should in any way be average, but rather that it should approach the ideal of an elegant or beautiful (*klanman*) neck—one slightly longer and finer than average and, if possible, with the highly desirable feature of beauty lines (*komin nglelie*).[16] These lines, or rings, around the neck are not folds of fat but rather slight creases horizontally aligned; such natural striation is recognized within the culture as inherently beautiful, a natural endowment complementing a neck already pleasing by its correct dimensions.[17] In sculpting figures, carvers often emphasize the neck by an unnatural length (as though they were expressing Brancusi's notion that in art the human neck can never be too long) and often idealize the neck rings by making them exceedingly regular and by making them entirely encircle the neck. This

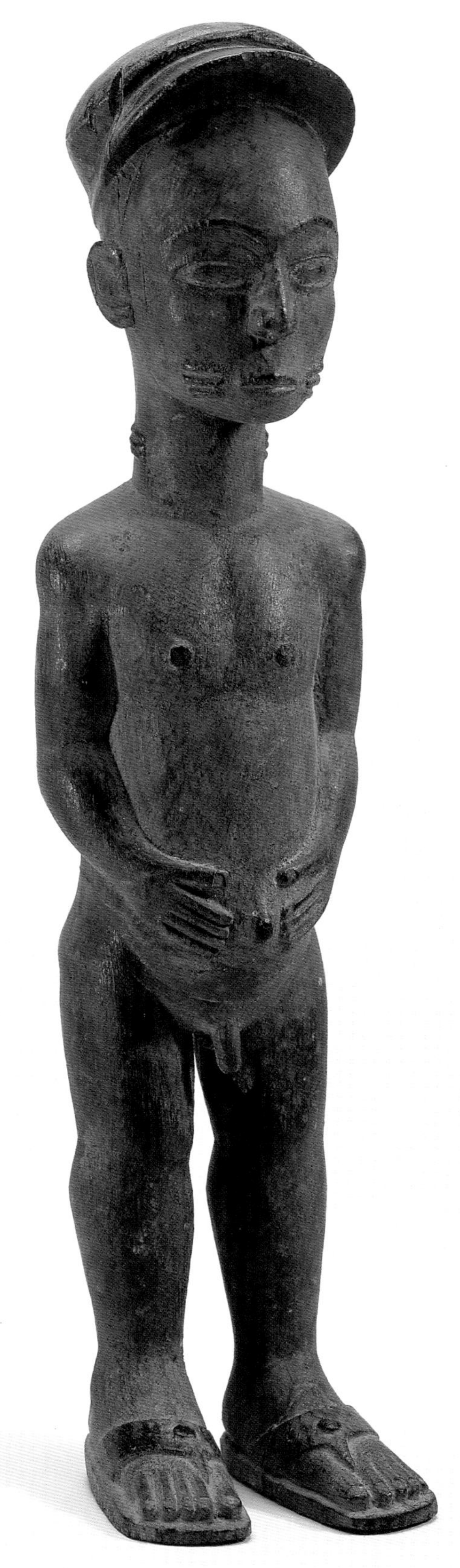

artistic idealization can serve in turn as a standard for aesthetic comparison, as when it is said of a person, "His neck is creased as though it were carved" (*i komin nglelie'n bubu ke b'a se i sa*).

The golden mean is also the operative aesthetic principle in relation to the dimensions of a person's (or a statue's) buttocks (*bondre*). They should be neither too developed ("like a northern woman's") nor too flat ("like a frog's"); rather, they should exhibit a correct roundness and firmness. The development of a girl's posterior during pubescence, like the development of her breasts, serves as a sign of her sexual maturity; her breasts and buttocks may now be squeezed in public flirting or caressed in private lovemaking (see Étienne 1972:70–71). The importance of the posterior may well be related to the definite association in Baule thought between buttocks and genitalia; the Baule word *bo*, which can be glossed as "bottom," "fundament," or "lower parts," includes those parts of the body that are referred to in English as "hips," "haunch," "buttocks," and "groin." *Bo* is thus the lower terminus of the trunk (*afien*), just as *ti* (head) is the upper terminus, and the two terms form an opposed pair, as in the proverb "A woman's bottom is more pleasing than her head" (*bla bo yo fe tre i ti*).[18]

In terms of mass and volume the head and bottom are linked to the torso (*afien*, "middle") but set off from it; the head is set off from the body by the neck (*komin*) and the bottom is set off by the pelvic circle (*bo nenglen*).[19] In translating this latter term as "pelvic circle," I mean to indicate the line of demarcation that passes immediately over the buttocks and follows the downward slope of the haunches toward the groin, that is, the natural line formed by the narrowing of the lower trunk and the bulge of the haunches (see ills. 1, 2, and 3). In traditional dress this line is emphasized by the beads and leather belts that men and women use respectively as cinctures that attach to their *cache-sexes*, or loincloths. The ensemble of the *cache-sexe* and the supporting girdle emphasizes the discontinuity between trunk and bottom. It also brings attention to the form of the buttocks, since the *cache-sexe*, in passing between the buttocks, makes obvious the fact that the posterior is made up of two separable masses.[20] Thus although the essential role of the *cache-sexe* is to cover the genitalia, it nonetheless also functions to reveal and accentuate the human form. In terms of traditional attitudes toward dress, a distinction must be made between the *cache-sexe* and the clothes worn by men and women as robes and wraps. The loincloth is of such importance that it is not considered to be fashion so much as the minimum requirement of modesty and, consequently, an unchanging given. Robes and wraps, which range from workaday practical dress to ceremonial formal finery, though governed by definite ideas of fashion, seem to be viewed as something added to the human body rather than as something used to transform the body.

2. Figure of an otherworld man wearing a billed cap and showing signs of having worn a cloth *cache-sexe*, c. 1940, height 31.5 cm. Fowler Museum of Cultural History, University of California, Los Angeles, X94.62.14.

There is a basic feeling that clothes, although used to cover, should not be

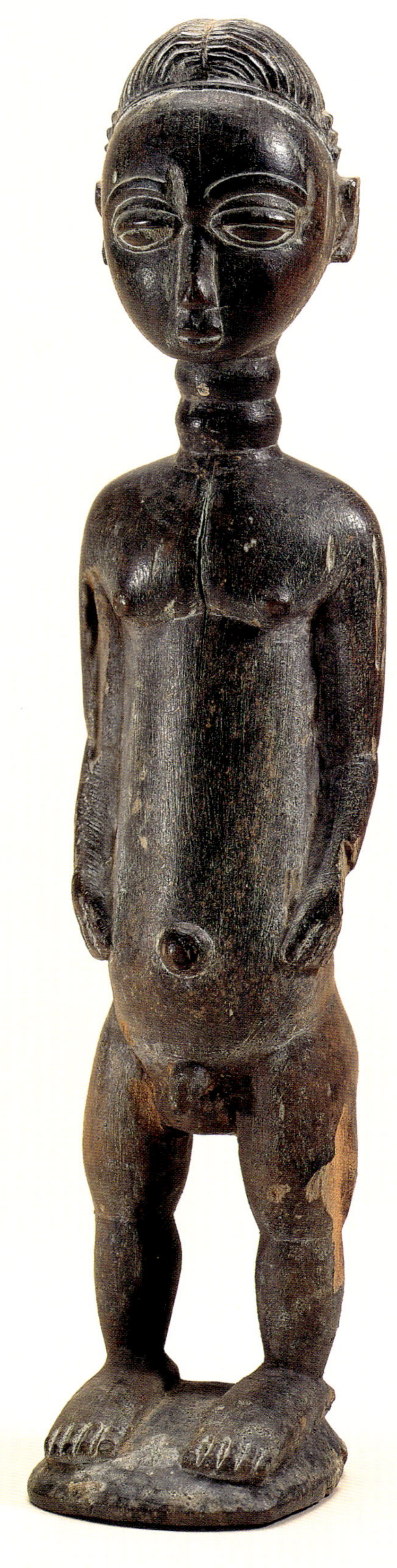

used to hide. A Baule proverb states, "One never knows when a northern woman is pregnant" (*be si'a kanga bla unzefue*), thus revealing the disapprobation with which the Baule view excessively voluminous dress The revelation of a person's physique is critically important throughout the years of adolescence. During this time, his or her character and abilities become apparent, and social identity starts to crystallize. A maiden's beauty is important for her marriageability, and a youth's form, particularly his musculature, is an indication of his adult potential.

This last point concerning male physique raises another aesthetic idea: in addition to quality (as revealed in the notion of the golden mean), there may also be definite ideas of plenitude. For example, there seems to be no such thing as excess musculature, since muscles are both a sign of character (having developed from physical labor) and a sure sign of future success. Thus the well-developed pectoral muscles found on male Baule statues indicate a social beauty that is quite different from the natural beauty of the gluteal muscles. The muscular development of the thighs and calves (especially on statues) is also seen in terms of physical splendor and strength. The shapeliness of muscular legs is appreciated not only for form but also for force. A typical appreciative comment regarding a man's legs is "His stance is good" (*i jran sue o ti kpa*); that is, he manifests stamina and solidity. Thus a comment on personal identity is couched in terms of form.

Understanding of the aesthetic of traditional statuary art among the Baule can only be achieved by an appreciation of the cultural eye with which human aesthetics are judged. The meaning of form in traditional Baule art can be found in the interrelations of these aesthetic frames of reference. Statuary form derives from an idealization of human form, and in turn sculptured ideals affect the appreciation of human beauty, as, for example, when one says, "His nose is as straight as though it were sculpted" (*i bue tinnge ke b'a se i sa*).

3. Figure of an other-world man with emphasized neck lines and prominent pectoral muscles; missing original cloth *cache-sexe*, c. 1925, height 31 cm. Fowler Museum of Cultural History, University of California, Los Angeles, X94.62.7.

Chapter Two

THE EFFECT OF FASHION ON FORM

Dress always characterizes certain social strata as belonging together; and it seems to fulfill this function best when it is imported from abroad. To dress as one does in Paris, means to have a close and exclusive association with a certain social strata in other countries—already the prophet Zephaniah speaks of noblemen as wearing foreign clothes.—George Simmel, *Conflict*

It is only through a study of emulation, and of the effect of revolutionary crises upon the emulative process, that we can understand fashion in its stages of critical development.—Quentin Bell, *On Human Finery*

The modernization of Baule statuary form by the introduction of Western-influenced clothes and attendant accessories such as shoes, hats, and watches has distressed some connoisseurs of so-called traditional African art in the same way that the use of modern clothes by the younger generation has distressed some Baule elders. The facile criticism of modern Baule statuary in pejorative terms finds an echo, for example, in the attitudes of some irascible old men who assume that young men wear modern dress simply to hide their physical faults, saying, "They take their skinny, scrawny legs and put them in pants." These attitudes—of the art critic and of the social critic—demonstrate a basic conservatism that would deny innovation and changing social realities; and the similarity of these views points out the relation between the aesthetics of art and the aesthetics of the artist's patrons. Michael Baxandall, writing on fifteenth-century Italian painting, states that certain artistic developments cannot be accounted for simply within the history of art; for example, the lessening preoccupation with precious pigments throughout the fifteenth-century was "part of a general movement in Western Europe at this time towards a kind of selective inhibition about display" (1972:14). I contend that the development of Baule figurative art throughout this century shows an increasing preoccupation with modern fashion that is part of a wider social

4. Figure of an other-world man wearing a billed cap, shirt, tie, shorts, belt, and saddle shoes, c. 1950, height 25 cm. National Museum of African Art, anonymous gift, 93-1-2.

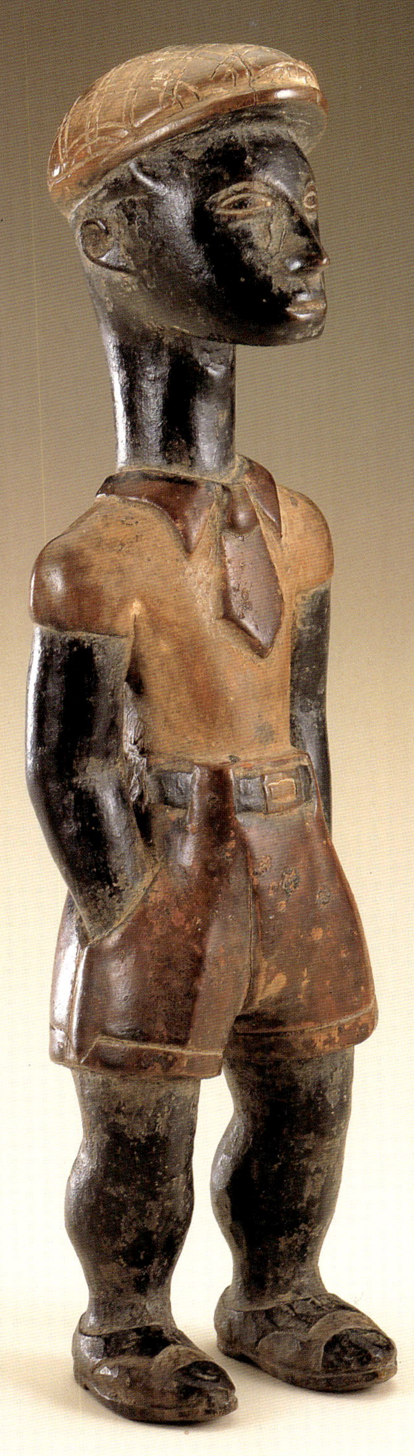

movement toward the exploitation of new cultural and technical forms introduced by the crisis of colonization—in brief, that Baule art exhibits the same emulative processes as the wider Baule society. We must recall that an otherworld mate is in a relation of opposition to the real-world spouse(s) or lover(s), that such a relation is characterized by mutual jealousy, and that the carving of a statue is undertaken for the purpose of appeasement. Furthermore, the form of the figure is governed by aesthetic canons directly related to those by which human beauty is judged. Thus our search for the meaning of modern accoutrements depicted in Baule art needs to take into account both the social significance of the cultural code of clothing and the use of this code in the individual sculptural representation of an otherworld mate in opposition to the perceptual attributes of an actual (or potential) real-world spouse.

THE DYNAMICS OF FASHION

The ethnographic study of clothing, like the structural analysis of phonology, investigates those elements in the system that, through opposition, convey meaning. The anthropologist looks at the differences in dress that follow conventionally established forms and thus serve to indicate marital status or to differentiate age classes, sociocultural classes, vocational groups, or townsmen from peasants (Trubetzkoy 1949:19). But how does one explain the introduction of new fashions into a traditional art form? The answer to this question lies in an understanding of the nature of the colonial society from which later Baule art derives its meaning. As Quentin Bell has stated, "In the history of man few things can be more important and few things will be found more characteristic of an age than the outward aspect of man himself" (1976:100).

It is important to understand the colonial society of Côte d'Ivoire holistically, to see the rulers and the ruled as parts of a whole rather than as two mutually opposed camps. The crisis of colonization introduced the Baule to a new society, hierarchically ordered. The highest level of this society was composed of the urban-dwelling foreign military and bureaucratic masters, and the lowest level, of the rural peasant masses. Between these two levels was interposed a burgeoning stratum of urban-oriented fortune hunters who sought livelihoods as entrepreneurs or salaried workers in the foreign bureaucratic government or military. This new, layered society was in turn linked to an international network centered in metropolitan France—a network that irrevocably changed Baule society by the communication of new technologies and new knowledge. This new order was controlled by armed power. Innovation was the result of imperialism, and change came about by the imposition of a new class system.

The imposition of the class system brought about a revolutionary crisis in the realm of dress. Dress became linked to fashion, whose mainspring is "the emulative process whereby the members of one class imitate those of another." Since fashion is "above all concerned with status" and its mechanisms "dependent upon the class structure of the society in which they operate" (Bell 1976:113, 117), we must look at the dress used in Baule statuary art as expressive of a fundamentally changed status system. The emulation that brought about a change in Baule fashion, with corollary changes in sculptural aesthetics, was an emulation of the new urban African. Thus a Baule statue in modern garb is neither a replica (Crownover 1960) nor a critical caricature (Lips 1937) of a European nor the expression of a wish for a European otherworld mate. Nor, finally, does the use of European dress or accoutrements mean that the art was conceived for a European market or that it panders to foreign clients.[1] Rather, it demonstrates a desire that the Baule otherworld mate exhibit those signs of success or status that characterize a white-oriented or -dominated society (see ills. 2, 4, 5, 8, 9, 10, 20, 25, 26). Although the artistic ideal begins to change with the introduction of new elements, especially of urban dress or the dress of "conspicuous leisure" (Bell 1976), the facial aesthetics of Baule statues remain relatively unchanged, as does the musculature of the limbs. That the use of European motifs is related to fashion as an emulative process has profoundly affected Baule society.

STATUARY FASHION AND CONJUGAL DYNAMICS

An insight into the dynamics of the fundamental triad of person, spouse, and otherworld mate (or perhaps one should say the double triad, since there is potentially a triad centering on each spouse) can be gained from a reading of Bell's discussion of "vicarious consumption," or "the display of sumptuosity through the agency of a third person" (1976:138–54). Bell uses this notion to discuss, for example, a wife's role of vicarious consumer for her husband, demonstrating on social or public occasions his ability to provide (pp. 139–40). No matter what individual psychological drives affect the lady's desire to dress up, a *social effect* is derived from the intent to demonstrate financial well-being. Similarly, in relation to Baule figures, while not denying the reality of certain psychological phenomena such as compensation for what is lacking in one's mate, we can nonetheless examine the social effects of status-laden dress. A good place to start this examination is with an actual case that forced me to investigate the real-world effects of an otherworld man having the identity of an *ancien combattant,* a veteran of the French army in foreign wars.

In francophone West Africa from the late 1940s through the 1970s, the image of the *ancien combattant* was one of a middle-aged man who, after having been forcibly conscripted to fight in World War II, had returned to his village with a pension and a boastful knowledge of the wider world.[2] Such a veteran often felt superior to others, and in the case of conflict with younger or less experienced people, he would assert that respect was due him for his age and experience, his typical refrain being "Moi, je connais . . . ," with the sense of "*I* know the wider world." His experiences often made him marginal to his natal group and consequently somewhat irascible and cantankerous, above all when taken lightly by a younger person. It was this image that came to mind when a young man told me in 1976 that his fiancée's *blolo bian* was an *ancien combattant* with a particularly quarrelsome nature. The young man, just starting his adult life after finding a job in town, was in the transitional period—the engagement (*soman*)—in which a man and a woman are official lovers, whether living together or not, but with the relationship of marriage not yet definitively established. During this period, compatibility is tested and interpersonal problems may be resolved. Thus when my young friend told me that his teenage fiancée had an otherworld man who was an *ancien combattant,* I was forced to reflect upon the significance of an age differential of twenty-five or more years between two men competing, as it were, for an attractive unmarried girl.

Given the adversarial, or at least oppositional, relation between an otherworld person and the spouse of his or her real-world mate, one can see that the imputation of a soldierly identification to one's otherworld man (especially when he is basically truculent) necessarily has an effect on the relation between husband and wife. The very existence of an otherworld mate permits a woman to maintain a certain individual identification; that is, her identity can never be totally subsumed into that of her husband, for he is not the only male who desires her. If, in addition, the otherworld mate of a woman exhibits qualities not to be found in her actual spouse, then this, too, serves as an inhibiting factor to her fiancé's or her husband's domineering tendencies as well as a demonstration of her independence. Conversely, the attributes of an otherworld woman, whether physically manifest in a statue or only talked about by her real-world man, affect the real-world marital relationship. The representation, for example, of her husband's otherworld woman as noticeably pregnant would undoubtedly create anxiety in a barren wife. Thus it is important to interpret the character ascribed to an otherworld mate in relation to the dynamics of the conjugal dyad. My analysis of the motifs found in Baule statuary art is that their meanings, like linguistic meanings, derive from contrast. What is important is the relative identity of a statue—the identity with which it is endowed in contrast to that of the real-world spouse with whom it is linked.

5. Figure of an otherworld man wearing a billed cap, shorts, ivory bracelet, amuletic armbands, pectoral amulet, and beaded necklace with a gold jewel, c. 1940, height 30 cm. Fowler Museum of Cultural History, University of California, Los Angeles, X94.62.26

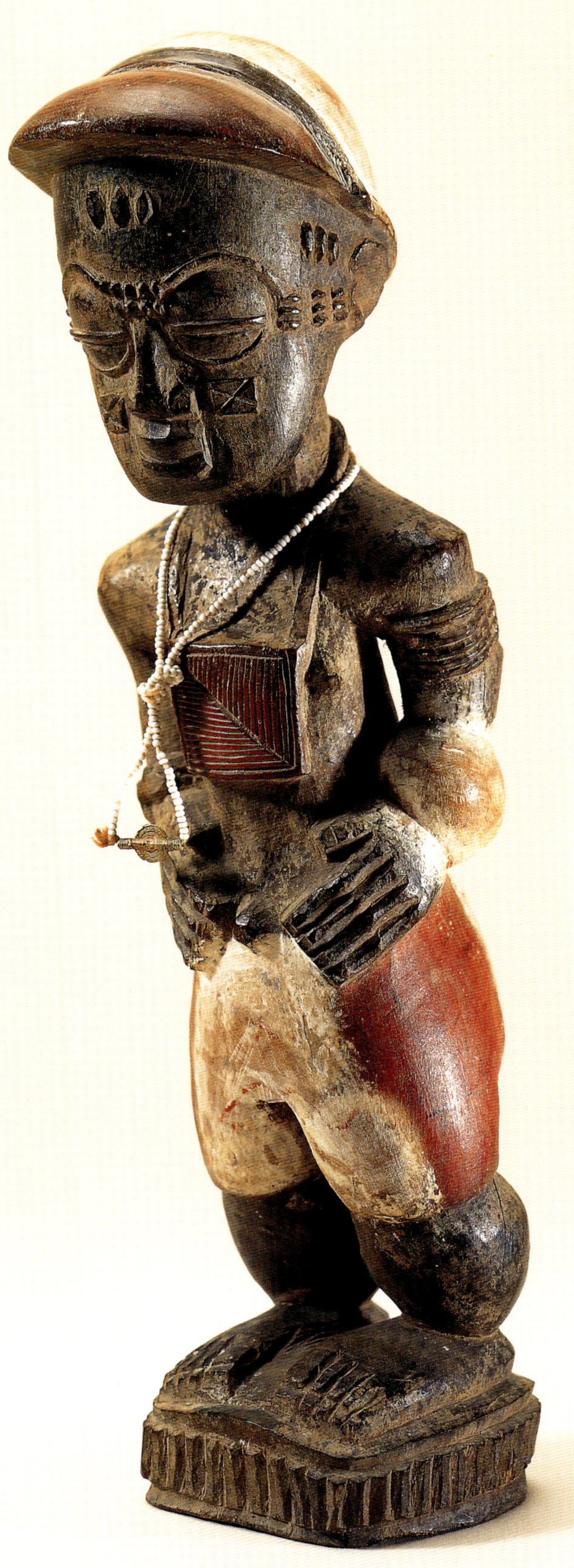

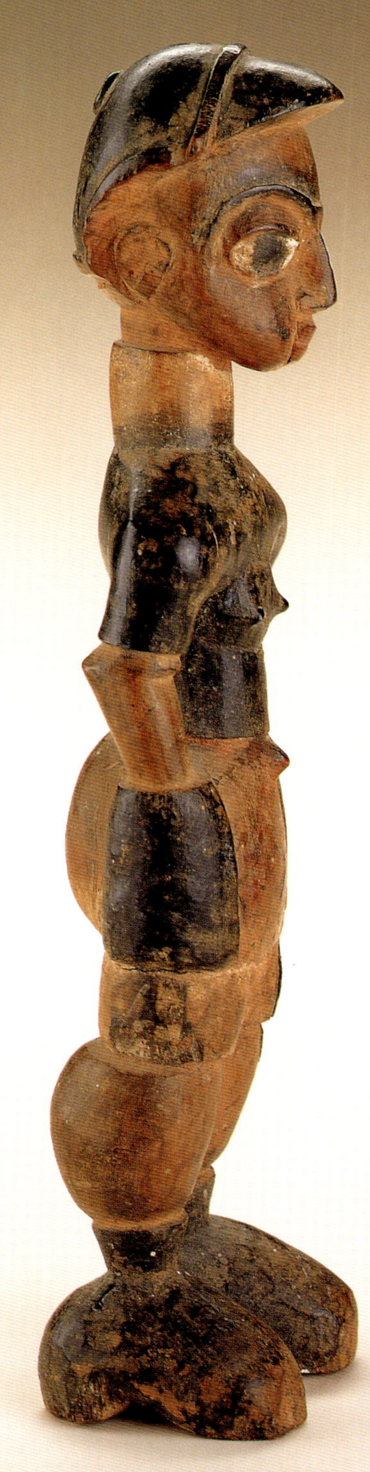

THE SIGNIFICANCE OF SCULPTURAL ELEMENTS

An inventory of the attributes of Baule statues that represent otherworld mates can be loosely organized in four categories: age, status, power, and individuality.

Age

In the 1970s if one had found a recently carved statue that represented a war veteran, one could have reasonably surmised that the otherworld man whom it represented was approximately fifty years old, although should one have come across a similar statue carved in the 1940s or 1950s, one could not have drawn the same conclusion. Thus without knowing the historical background of particular statues, one must be careful about interpreting such signs of relative age. Certain motifs, however, may be used to infer an intended absolute age in the representation of spirit mates, for example, the use of a beard on a statue, whether traditional or modern (see ill. 19). Since beards are in theory limited to old men (*kpenngben*) and since a statue is supposed to be a faithful representation of the characteristics of an otherworld mate, one is justified in concluding that the otherworld man is not just an adult but also an elder, a *doyen.*[3] Another indicator of absolute age is the positioning or form of breasts on female statues. High, firm breasts may indicate that the otherworld woman thus depicted is a maiden (*talua*) who has not borne children; fuller or more sagging breasts may indicate a woman of childbearing age or in the early stage of pregnancy; and flattened breasts, although rarely depicted, could be a sign that the otherworld woman has already borne numerous children.

Status

It is especially in modern figures that social position may be made manifest. The dress of a gendarme, a bureaucrat, or a town dweller gives an unambiguous indication that the spirit mate whom it represents is perceived as an active participant in the modern world. The use of shoes, suits, ties, and other fashion items creates a social identity of success, either the success of urban employment or the success of a farmer who is sufficiently rich to use urban dress for his leisure. Bearing in mind that this identity is relational, one may easily imagine the dynamics between a woman and her poor farmer husband who is confronted with an otherworld competitor exhibiting signs of urban material success. Likewise, one may imagine the psychological position of a sterile woman when the *blolo bla* of her husband is physically represented with a nursing child. The possible indicators of social status are almost limitless: a rifle may signal the highly coveted role of hunter, a ceremonial cane may convey high status, or—and this is an example based on an actual figure that brought great renown to its carver in the Baule village of Bourébo in

6. Figure of an otherworld man wearing a billed cap, shorts, shirt, and shoes. The pectoral muscles show through the painted-on shirt, c. 1950, height 24 cm. Private collection. Photograph by Franko Khoury.

the sous-préfecture of Béoumi—a typewriter may demonstrate the secretarial vocation of an otherworld woman.

Power

Some indicators of personal power—readily perceived by the cultural eye but somewhat less evident to the outsider—are the various amulets such as armbands (*banzre*), bracelets (*blenga*), rings (*nga*), necklaces and waistbands (*sebe*), and leg bands (*ja nyama*) that may be carved on figures. Each of these amulets indicates that the wearer possesses a special power derived from a spiritual agency. In addition to being the repository of this power, the amulet may also serve as a signal to others to be careful in their actions toward the bearer. The amassing of amulets (ill. 5) signals an additional hazard because it is often thought a difficult task to harmonize their talismanic powers. Furthermore, since each amulet entails specific taboos, the accumulation of amulets means an increasing difficulty in respecting them all and avoiding madness. Once again we see the social effect of costume and again we are forced to reflect on the effect of such a motif when found on the sculpted representative of a third party to a marriage. A statue may express other powers as well, whether physical, political, or fecund. In this regard, while modern dress is increasingly important, the emphasis on physique is still evident, and dress may be purposely revealing, as when a painted shirt clings to an imposing chest (ill. 6).

Individuality

One of the primary requirements of a statue representing an otherworld mate is that it exhibit his or her peculiar characteristics, that is, his or her particular individuality. Notwithstanding the similarities of style that result from the culturally defined artistic tradition, or those that are due to the specific hand of the artist, a statue should ideally portray a unique ensemble of features. Given this necessary demonstration of individuation, one can see that the introduction of new fashion items enlarges the corpus of diagnostic criteria that the artist uses to particularize a figure. If one takes several examples of a single artist's work, one can observe unique combinations of elements, even though certain similarities of artistic interpretation remain constant (Ravenhill 1981:129–30). Whereas the basic forms of the sculptures may be comparable and exhibit the carver's characteristic touch, the carver may introduce idiosyncrasy by adding, omitting, or modifying such features as headgear, coiffure, clothing, scarification, ornamentation, fashion accoutrements, or footwear. The use of dyes or other coloring agents such as kaolin, not to mention the current use of commercial paints, also allows a greater variety of presentation. In sum, a Baule carver of images of otherworld mates is somewhat like a portraitist in the Western tradition of art in that his task is to present a faithful portrayal of the character of an individual (Read 1931:33f), and in order to realize "the personality of his subject in its uniqueness" (p. 34), he makes full use of the motifs and features discussed above.

THE EVOLUTION OF SCULPTURE

Implicit in the preceding discussion is the idea of the continuity of an artistic tradition. In examining the dynamics of the tradition's evolution, my concern has been to avoid that "static definition of social life" which is "one of the dangers constantly threatening a sociology of art" (Duvignaud 1972:142). Thus rather than looking at traditional art as a past stage of development that is to be contrasted to a later stage of modernism, I have attempted to view recent innovations in terms of amplification and perdurability. The art has changed, as has the society in which it is produced, but the new has not replaced the old but rather transformed it. Let us now look at several changes of sculptural form from an art-theory point of view.

One significant difference between clothed and unclothed Baule statues is to be found in the interpretation of the trunk of the body. Traditionally the trunk (*afien,* "middle") is interpreted artistically as a single unit bounded by the neck and the *bo nenglen* (pelvic circle), that is, as the total middle mass between the head (*ti*) and the bottom (*bo*).[4] With the introduction of clothing, however, the interpretation of the trunk often emphasizes the division of the trunk into chest (*we*) and belly (*ku*) by making explicit the waist (although there is no Baule word for waist).[5] In traditional thought, the chest and belly are seen as the upper and lower parts of the trunk but with no particular line of division between the two. Unlike the Western notion of "waist," which has the sense of a circular narrowing of the trunk on a horizontal plane whether seen from the front or the side, the Baule notion of *bo nenglen,* does not refer to the trunk at all but rather to a line between the trunk and the composite of hips, haunches, and groin. This line, when seen from the side, descends at an approximately thirty-degree angle from the horizontal. The carving of a waist not only does away with the *bo nenglen* but also drastically changes the profile by a strictly horizontal division of the body. This division of the body owes more to fashion than to physique. The idea of a waist, therefore, must be seen as cultural rather than natural. The waist has a tenuous relation to physical form, as is only too evident when one reads Bell's *On Human Finery* (1976). In describing various eras of fashion, Bell refers to waists that are pinched-in, thick, broad, nonexistent, natural, distorted, or even "a few inches below the arm pits" (pp. 66, 83, 158, 156, 163, 175, 166, 214).[6] Thus the introduction of the Western notion of waist into Baule statuary art (see ills. 4, 7, 16, 20, 21, 25) has had the immediate effect of transforming the idea of bodily volume, of demonstrating the maxim that clothes do indeed make the man.

Some of the other elements developed in recent Baule figurative art have more direct antecedents in traditional forms. Take, for example, the positioning of the arms and hands. With traditional Baule statues there is a general tendency for the arms either to closely follow the form of the trunk or to be sculpted directly on it in low relief, and concurrently for the hands to be minimal and in a position of rest on either side of the navel (see ills. 1, 2, 3, 9). In more recent clothed statues the arms are often in the same relative position, the upper arms hanging more or less straight down by the sides, and the forearms coming toward the front of the body, but the hands *tend* to be placed, or perhaps one should say hidden, in pockets (see ills. 4, 6, 7, 16, 20, 21, 26). Thus the idea continues in modified form; arms that formerly terminated in diminutive hands now end in pockets, as though the Baule sculptor had decided that the final solution to the problem of hands was to do away with them entirely.

The importance of the head is a constant in old and newer forms of Baule art. For example, there is virtually no difference in the proportion of the head to the body; both earlier and later forms manifest a disproportionate emphasis on the head. This is due, perhaps, to the importance of the face and gaze in the recognition of the figure's personhood (see chap. 4) and in the perception of individual identity, as well as the special significance of facial aesthetics in the overall consideration of human beauty.

One seemingly major contrast between traditional and modern statues is that of coiffure versus headgear, but the similarities of purpose are greater than any superficial differences. One of the most important functions of human hair is that of social indicator; the coiffing or shaving of hair is undertaken for such social ends as the marking of a change in status, as in bereavement, or the demonstration of social proprieties (Hallpike 1969). Coiffure makes manifest, so to speak, tonsorial morality; the person who is properly coiffed implicitly acknowledges allegiance to prevalent social standards. Similarly, in Baule figurative art, coiffure indicates the social character of the otherworld person who is represented; the artist makes use of culturally ordained aesthetic criteria to demonstrate the humanness and individual identity of the spirit mate. Given that the "head is always a most sensitive index of fashionable change" (Bell 1976:123), it is not surprising that sculptural innovation makes ready use of imported headgear and new tonsorial fashions. The colonial pith helmet, one of the most important symbols of raw political power during the early colonial era, became one of the most common accoutrements represented in Baule figurative art of that period (see ills. 8, 23, 27). More recently the representation of headgear seems to have decreased in importance in direct relation to the expanding importance of the new hairstyles that have originated in the urban context. The new styles, publicized

7. Figure of an otherworld man wearing shoes and colonial-era uniform, and with a barbershop hairstyle and facial scarification, c. 1950, height 37 cm. Fowler Museum of Cultural History, University of California, Los Angeles, X94.62.8.

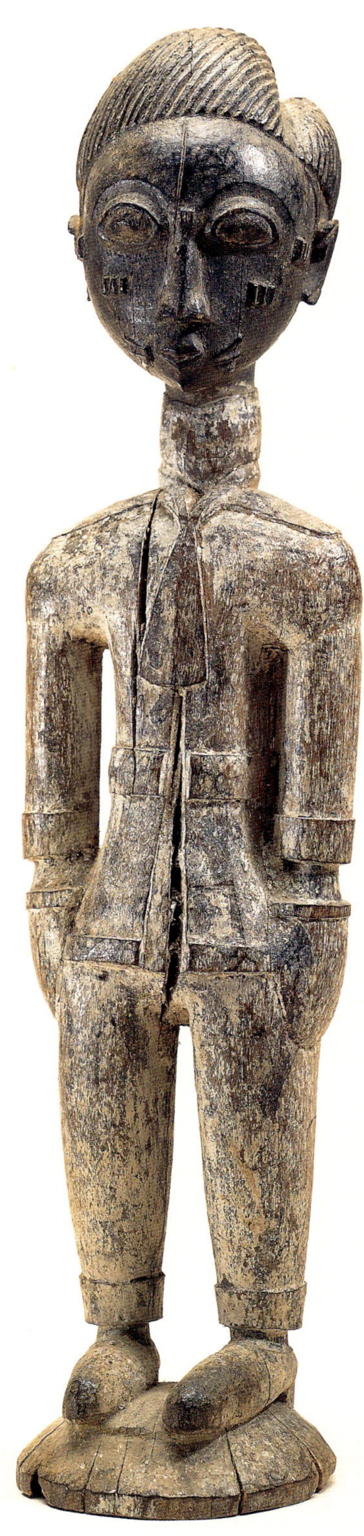

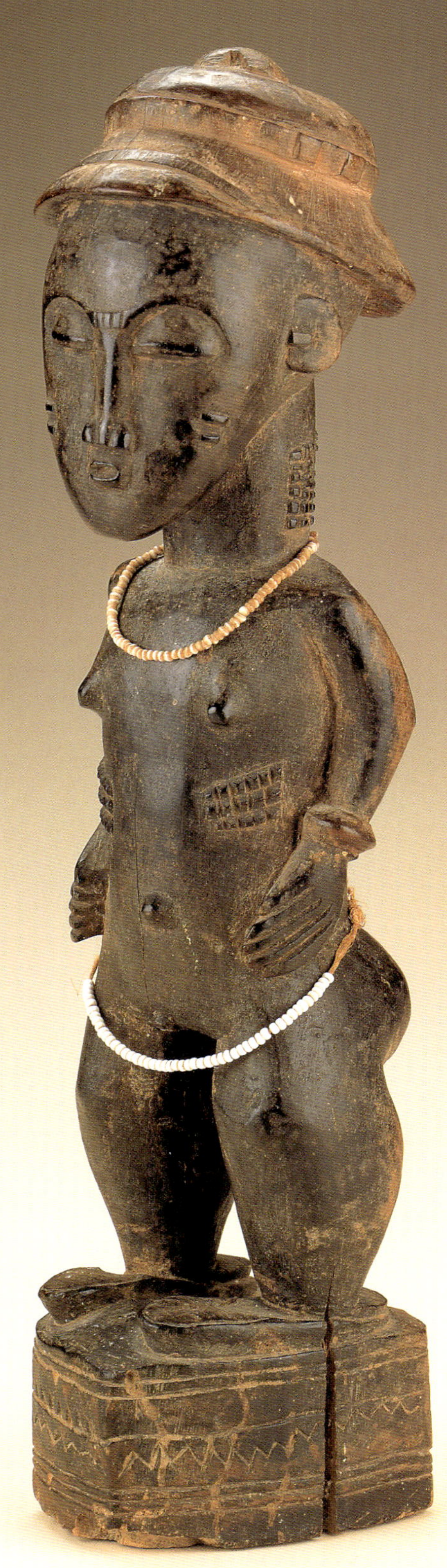

by barbershop signs and bearing such exotic names as Ghana, Pélé (after the Brazilian football star), Babyface, Azazou, Yéyé, Santiago, or even Ordinaire, are symbols par excellence of the developing urban aesthetic in the postcolonial nation-state. The incorporation of these new hairstyles into Baule art demonstrates the dynamism of the artistic tradition and, once again, the continuous interrelation of human and sculptural aesthetics (ill. 9).

Scarification, both facial and corporal, also has a modern equivalent, both in Baule society and sculpture: dandification. Traditionally the Baule associated scarification with youth, the time between childhood and adulthood during which the Baule expect that youths will "do their young man thing" (*di gbanflen*) and maidens will "do their young woman thing" (*di talua*), that is, enjoy their physical maturity before accepting the constraints of adulthood and social maturity. This time of life is critical for the presentation of self, since it is at this time that one forms one's social identity and that one's public character becomes known. Just as it is possible to take or be given a youth nickname (*gbanflen dunman* or *talua dunman* for males and females respectively) that characterizes this incipient social identity, so scarification was undertaken to affect one's image by the permanent addition of signs of beauty.[7] Clothes now function for image building in the same way that scars once did, although, obviously, clothes are a more flexible means of social transformation.

The similarities between traditional and modern Baule art are much more significant than the differences. There has been no radical disjunction in the art's evolution; the new flows naturally from the old with the function remaining the same, even though the form takes advantage of new elements, especially those of dress.

CLOTHED MEN AND UNCLOTHED WOMEN

My observations of the art market in the town of Bouaké have indicated not only a significant disproportion in the ratio of male to female statues but also a similar disproportion in the incidence of clothing on male and female statues. Based on personal observations, I would state that a male statue has a far higher probability of being clothed than a female. If one can assume that my observations in the Côte d'Ivoire art market over a period of fifteen years (1972–87) accurately reflect the reality of statue and motif distribution, then we are faced with the question of why male statues demonstrate modernism more frequently than do female statues.

A possible partial explanation of this disparity could be found in the fact that modern female dress shows less difference from traditional dress than does modern male dress and, thus, that there is no disruptive change in female fashion to capitalize on in figurative art. Or one might assume that mod-

8. Figure of an other-world man wearing a colonial-era pith helmet, slip-on shoes, beaded necklace, and hip beads, c. 1920, height 32.5 cm. National Museum of African Art, anonymous gift, 93-1-1.

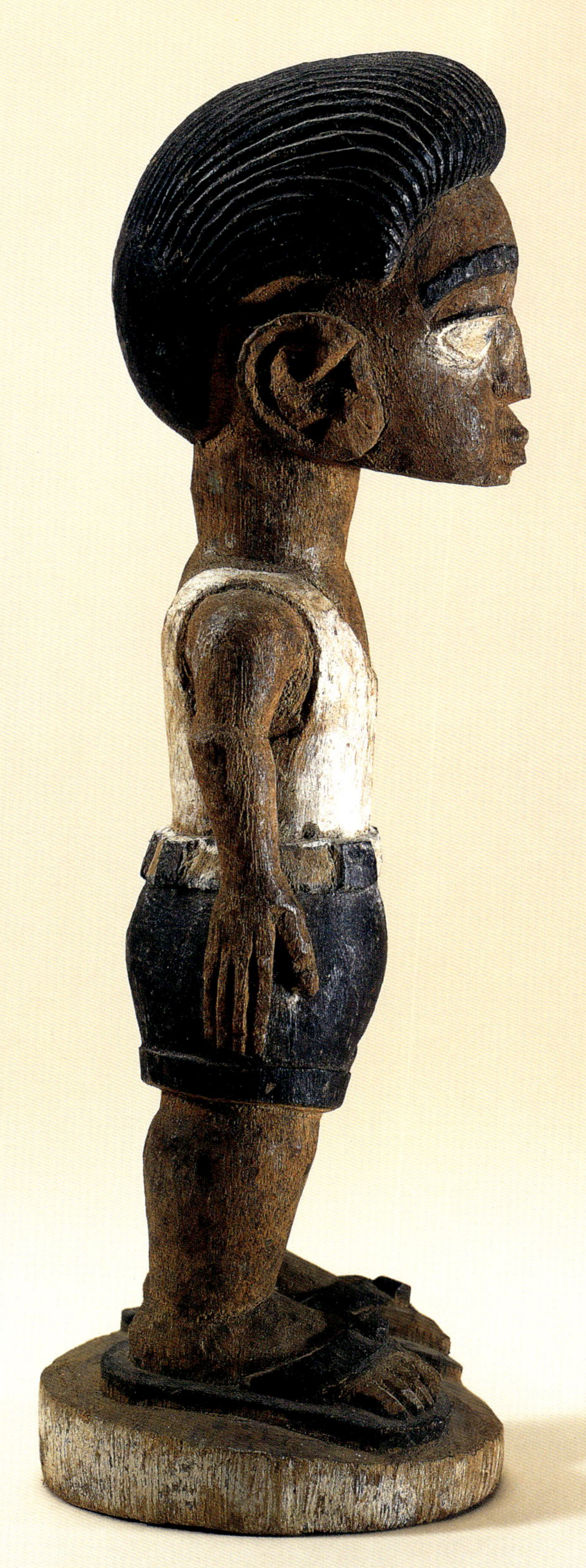

ern roles for women show significantly less difference from traditional roles than do modern roles for men and, thus, that the modern artistic interpretation of women has more limited possibilities. Another way of looking at this issue, however, would be to examine basic differences between the social positions of the two sexes.

One very significant gender-based difference in Baule society is that it is indisputably easier for a woman to get a husband than it is for a man to get a wife. No matter what her problems may be, it is exceedingly rare for a woman who desires marriage to remain unmarried; such is not the case for a man, and many men spend years of difficulty before finding a wife. In addition, a woman has more choices in acquiring a marital partner than does a man. Whereas a woman can usually choose from among many suitors, a man may be practically forced to accept the single alternative imposed upon him by factors of availability beyond his control. Thus, in the contemporary situation, the criteria that a woman uses in the selection of a spouse are more social than physical. For a man, however, the criteria are less social than physical. In other words, for a man the emphasis is on the physical potential of the woman he chooses for his wife, since above all he needs her for her capacity to bear children. It is perhaps this difference of expected roles (social versus natural) that is echoed in the difference of depiction of clothing on male and female statues.[8]

The difference between clothed male statues and unclothed female statues could also be due to the difference of the impact that towns had on Baule men and women during the colonial era. As the Étiennes (1968) point out, a town, as the seat of colonial power, functioned as a pole of repulsion for men but as a pole of attraction and refuge for women.[9] Thus the openness of women toward an urban existence may find an echo in the urban image of their otherworld men, whereas men's otherworld women preserve in their statuary form the dress and appearance of the more traditional rural sector.

9. Figure of an otherworld man wearing a pompadour hairstyle, tank top, shorts, belt, and sandals, c. 1955, height 28 cm. Fowler Museum of Cultural History, University of California, Los Angeles, X94.77.4.

Chapter Three

DREAMS, REVERIE, AND INDIVIDUAL EXISTENCE

In spite of my past avoidance of any psychological investigation of Baule images of otherworld mates, I remain keenly interested in the psychology of both individual and social meaning, the reality of the individual's experience of art within a particular cultural and social matrix. Beyond art as a social construct of its culture of origin and art as the art historian's datum of investigation, is there not place for another type of examination of art and the individual? And if so, how does one begin to explore the place, the character, the affectivity, the reality, the efficacy, and the effect of art in individual experience?

Much has been written in recent years about whether or not art is simply a Western construct and thus an idea that is not applicable to the artifacts of other societies. It is argued that these societies have no word for art and that, therefore, what the Westerner appropriates as art is *in situ* an entirely different kind of thing. Indeed, some artifacts become appropriated as art only because of their formal similarity to Western works of art, even if such appropriation suffers from a tendency toward anachronism. For example, in looking at nineteenth-century Kalabari ancestral screens, we perceive them with eyes conditioned by twentieth-century notions of collage and assemblage, and we easily, yet somewhat ethnocentrically, see and claim them as universally valid, marvelous works of art that intrigue us because of their liminal existence between two and three dimensions (Ravenhill and Walker 1988). In our own individual and social constructions of reality, we would like to be able to categorize confidently an object as either art or artifact, and keep our minds tidy with the proper separation between the two. We would like to think that we know when an object *is* art.

I would affirm, rather than deny, the cross-cultural appeal of art—leaving aside for the moment any attempt at defining that word—and yet I am most uncomfortable with our implicit imposition of Western notions of aesthetics onto the art of other people. I am also not at ease with the facile assumption

10. Figure of an otherworld man wearing a sharply defined modern suit and hairstyle, dress shirt, tie, and shoes, c. 1960, height 33.6 cm. Fowler Museum of Cultural History, University of California, Los Angeles, X94.18.2.

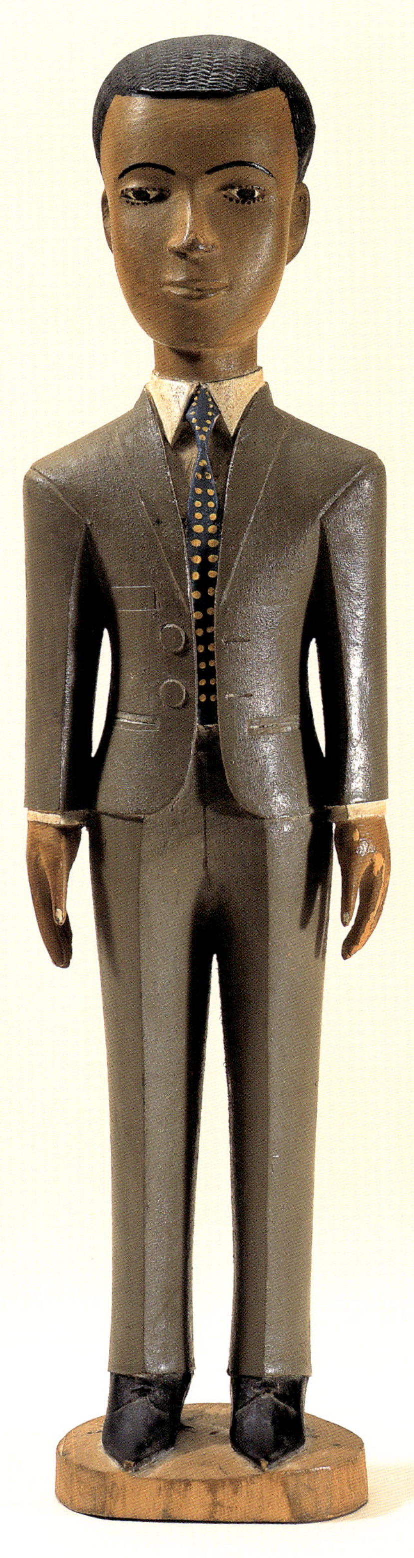

that art *is* something that one can readily recognize. The problem is that if we limit our discourse to the *what* of art—its visually perceived formal qualities—then we can easily ignore the fundamental questions of the *why* and the *how* of the work of art in its original intentionality, creation, and experience.

In thinking about my own observations of other people's experience of art, especially among the Wan[1] and Baule of Côte d'Ivoire, I have finally found myself musing far less about what art is than about what it does. In talking about art with those who commission it, those who create it, and those who use it, one often learns things of interest that add to an understanding of at least some of the aspects of the art itself. The procedure of cultural exegesis in the study of art relies heavily on what is *said* about art, but ultimately one must admit that art has a power far beyond words.

Art is powerful because it is another form of knowledge, communication, and experience. As such, it does things that otherwise cannot be done. It has an individual reality and ontological status, or autonomy, that is independent of the anthropologist's or art historian's categorization, idealization, or explanation. Art is even independent of any interpretation offered by its maker. Art, the created object, can be confrontational. It can create, in the words of Michael Brenson, "a bodily encounter" in the viewer.

> The type of encounter I am talking about is a concentration of psychological, philosophical, artistic, and political information that is impossible to reduce. The contact is physical. Its breath of thoughts and feelings is accepted and taken in by the body which always knows more than the mind can grasp. (1992:15)

Ignoring the confrontational, active power of art, the scholar examining art cross-culturally often resorts to the construction of ideal or abstract categories as a way to come to grips with unusual phenomena in a foreign culture. In so doing, he or she often unintentionally overstates the case being described, positing distinctions and articulating models that are in fact idealized intellectual constructs totally abstracted not only from the vagaries and realities of individual experience but also from any understanding of their affective power. From an acquired understanding of cultural concepts and constitutive rules of behavior, the scholar delivers assertions about typical notions or generalized norms that are implied to be culturally valid and uniformly true. The gap, however, that exists between such social *facts* (that theoretically pertain to an entire culture) and the personal or psychological *experiences* of specific individuals within the culture is enormous. The two realities—abstractly constructed and psychologically experienced—are worlds apart.

Let me relate two experiences. In 1982, after almost ten years of residence in Côte d'Ivoire and after having researched Baule art for a number of years, I worked with Stéphan Kurc, a French filmmaker, on a series of films, *Dialogue*

11. Figure of an other-world woman belonging to a wandering minstrel. Photographed in a village chief's guest room alongside the minstrel's guitar and dance costume. Tiébissou region, Côte d'Ivoire, 1982. Photograph by Lap Nguyen Tien.

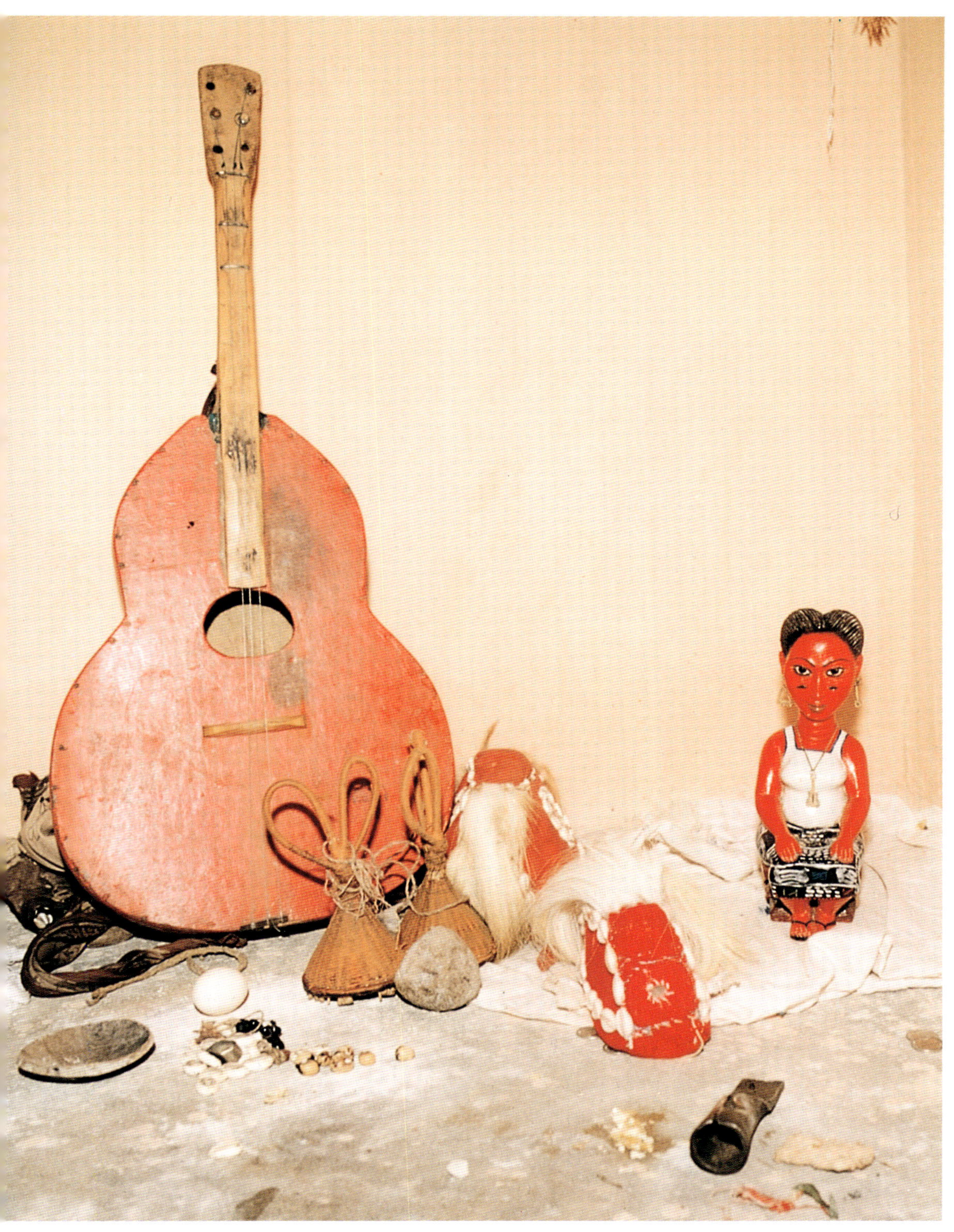

avec le sacré, that explored traditional Ivorian arts. While filming in a Baule village for *Les Amants de l'au-delà: La Statuaire baoulé* (1982), I had two experiences that revealed to me the profound difference between a scholar's understanding of cultural facts and the insider's internalized knowledge that yields the immediacy of affective reality.

We had decided to conduct a number of unrehearsed on-camera interviews for the film, asking people to talk about their experiences with either their own or their spouse's otherworld man or woman. At the end of the first interview with a man and his two co-wives, I called the film crew purser over, saying, "Cinq milles, cinq milles"—the conventional Ivorian manner of saying "Five thousand [francs] each." Both the purser (a non-Baule) and I assumed that we had a total outlay of fifteen thousand francs, that is, five thousand francs times three. After each of the interviewees was paid, however, the husband quietly but firmly said, "And my otherworld woman?" For him, but not for me, she was as real and as worthy of reward as he and his two real-world wives.[2]

I subsequently returned to the same village with the photographer Lap Nguyen Tien to shoot Baule statuettes *in situ* (Ravenhill 1985). We were able to photograph a number of statuettes that had previously been filmed, and in addition we were invited to photograph the statuette (*waka sran*) of an itinerant guitar-playing minstrel who was in temporary residence as an evening performer. In the spare and well-swept guest quarters of the village chief, where he was staying, we found a sleeping mat, a red guitar, a dance costume, and a statuette (ill. 11). In talking to the minstrel, it became evident that although he referred to the female figure as his *blolo bla,* she was also the one who inspired his public performances and he therefore displayed her during them. His performance costume (short skirt, cowrie-shell bandoliers, and plumed leather cap) was directly analogous to that worn by Baule trance diviners (*komienfwe*), whom bush spirits possess and endow with clairvoyance (Ravenhill 1994:23f). Comparably sculpted figures also represent these spirits, and the diviner usually displays them during his or her public performances (ills. 12, 13).

My reality, in which I thought I understood an idealized set of oppositional categories (otherworld figures versus bush-spirit figures), was confronted by *his* reality in which a muselike otherworld being empowered his performances—a being whose attributes seemed to merge those of my two ideal types. My constructed facts met a different psychological reality, and I was obliged to look at the guitar pendant necklace on the figure in a different light (ill. 14). I now saw beyond the figure's guitar as miniature musical instrument to the instrumentality of the otherworld woman in the minstrel's music.

12. *Asie usu* figure belonging to a trance diviner. Tiébissou region, Côte d'Ivoire, 1981. Photograph by Lap Nguyen Tien.

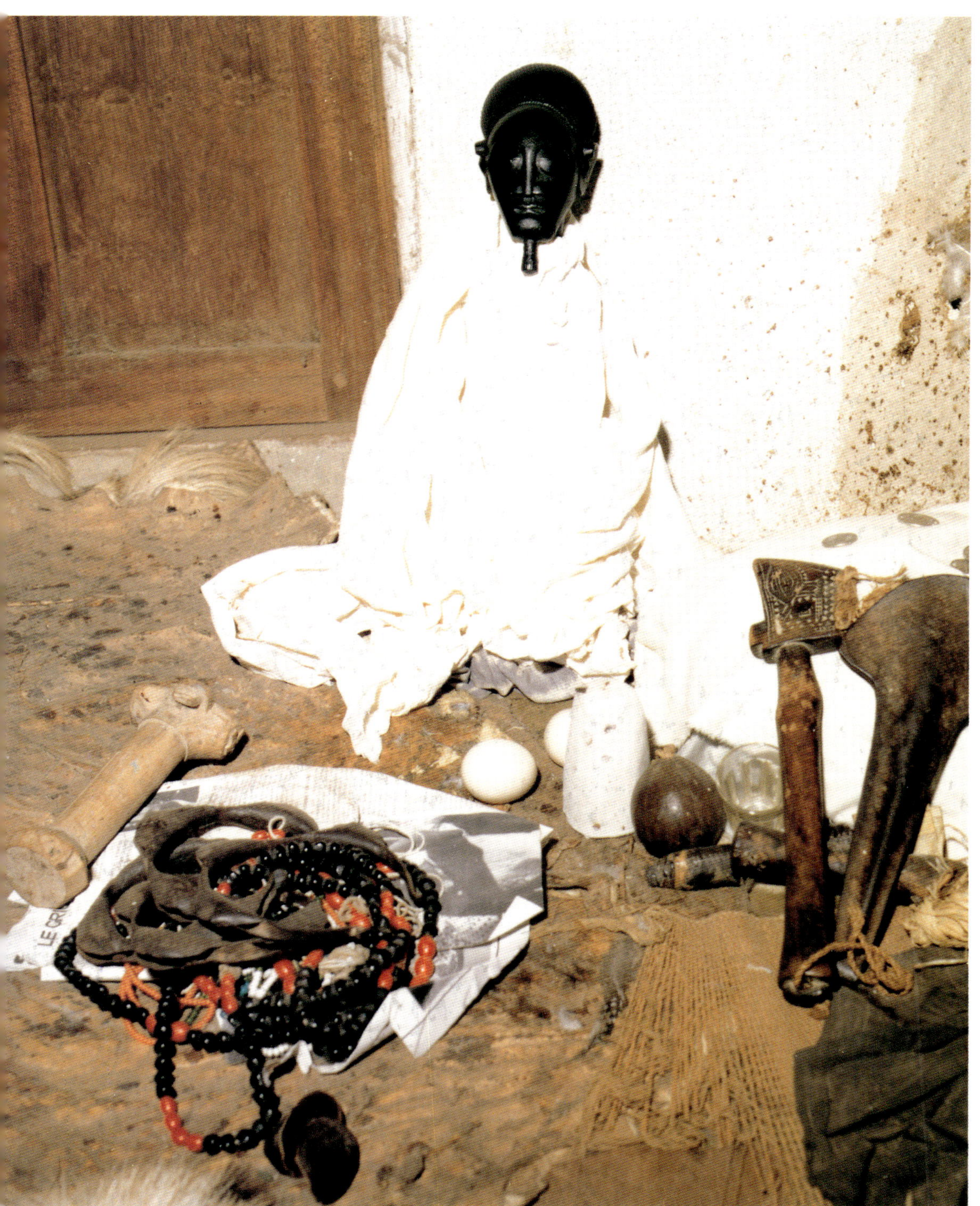

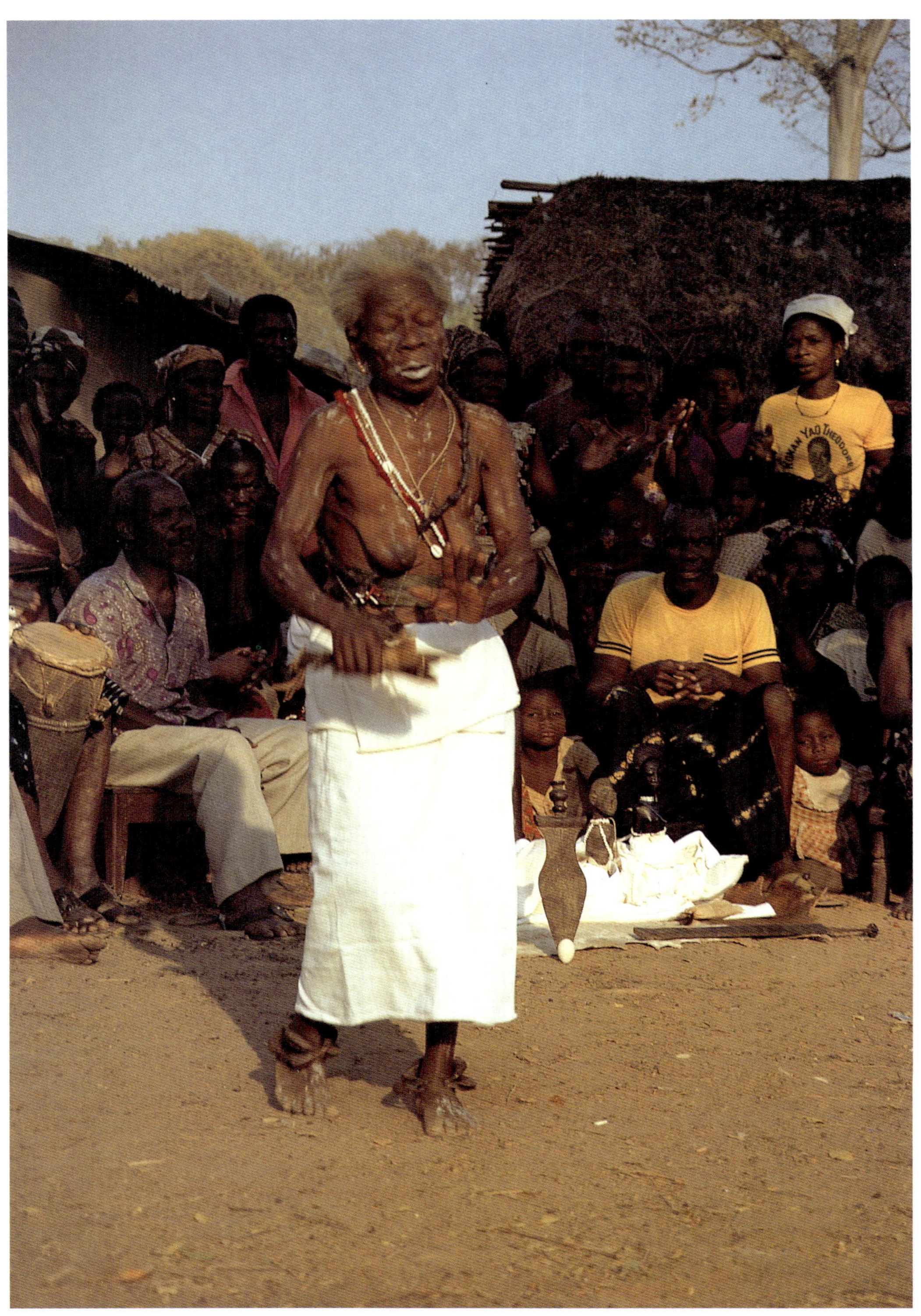

ART AND DREAMED EXPERIENCE

In terms of the individual's experience of art, one of the fascinating aspects of Baule otherworld figures is that they represent beings who are encountered only in dreams. The existence and experience of the otherworld and the otherworld mate are confirmed through both divination and dreams. Artists carve statuettes to "bring down" (*jra*), to "create," or concretize, the otherworld partner in response to a real-life crisis. When an artist receives a commission, the form and character of the otherworld being can be based either on the pronouncements of the diviner or on firsthand description obtained from the client's vivid dreams of the otherworld mate. Direct knowledge of the otherworld person is not, however, limited to the diviner or the client. It is also quite common for a real-world spouse or sexual partner to see and experience this *blolo* person in his or her dreams. And the artist himself can dream of the form of this otherworld mate during the weeks that it takes him to carve its physical representation.

As mentioned earlier, when one dreams of one's *blolo* mate, the mate may have a constant form or may variously assume the appearance and identity of any actual person with the important exception of one's physical mate. This contrastive or competitive identity is also confirmed by the rule (socially expected and specifically confirmed as part of the diviner's revelations) that an appointed night of the week be set aside for the dream visit of the otherworld mate. On that night one cannot sleep or have sexual relations with a real-world partner. Instead one has dreams, often sexual, that involve the otherworld person and create consciousness. "Whatever else happens during dream formation, dreaming is a 'becoming conscious.' It is a lived experience, potentially full of an immediately sensed felt meaning" (Hunt 1989:209). It is this inward, lived experience of the dreamworld that is externalized and reified in the commissioned sculpture, a carving that not only depicts idealized human beauty but also the physical, social, and characteristic attributes of a specific individual.

The physical form of the statuette undoubtedly has an effect on future dreamings, in that it may serve to canalize attitudes and feelings. Harry Hunt has argued that "there is considerable indication that dreams can be socially malleable and patterned—that dream formation can become part of an ongoing dialogic process" (1989:12). Indeed, Baule expectations that dreams *will* occur every week on the designated night are a prime example of what Hunt refers to as "*dream incubation* in which specific sorts or dreams are deliberately sought" (emphasis added).

13. *Komien* dancer performing, with *asie usu* figures on display. Tiébissou region, Côte d'Ivoire, 1981. Photograph by the author.

A commonly held Western assumption is that dream projections and performances are the means whereby the unconscious seeks to resolve psychological problems that remain unresolved in the conscious mind, that is, "that dreams result from a competition between a coherent organizing system . . . and a more primitive and ultimately disruptive tendency" (Hunt 1989:ix–x). In this, our own post-Freudian, conflict-resolution model of dreaming, the unconscious is the internal driving force that imposes its dreams upon the dreamer. The Baule view of reality, however, is that *blolo* dreaming is always initiated from the outside, that is, by the *blolo* mate. Nonetheless, the dreaming is implicitly encouraged. One goes to bed expecting to dream of a specific and *real* person, thereby instituting and maintaining an ongoing, permanent relationship. The dreamworld, furthermore, is reified and incorporated into the day-to-day world of marital or sexual dynamics. The otherworld person is a *real* rival. And through art, he or she is manifested *physically* as a carved figure, another presence in the conjugal bedroom.

Gaston Bachelard, in his study *The Poetics of Reverie* (1971), wonders

> whether there really is a consciousness of dreams. A dream can be so strange that it seems that another subject has come to dream within us. "A dream visited me." That is certainly the formula which indicates the passivity of great nocturnal dreams. To convince ourselves that they are really ours, we must reinhabit these dreams. Afterwards we make up accounts of them, stories from another time, adventures from another world. (P. 11)

For the Baule dreamer the actively remembered nighttime dream of the *blolo* is incorporated into lived experience by becoming in the light of day a narrative. "It is in the way we spontaneously handle dreams on awakening that finishes the operation by turning the dream into a story" (Hunt 1989:178). Week by week, the stories and their dramatic dialogue become the basis for further personal musings. The reinhabited dreams make possible reverie, a cosmic reverie.

> Cosmic reveries separate us from project reveries. They situate us in a world and not in a society. . . . Through the cosmicity of an image then, we receive an experience of the world; cosmic reverie causes us to inhabit a world. It gives the dreamer the impression of a home (*chez soi*) in the imagined universe. The imagined world gives us an expanding *home*, the reverse of the *home* of the bedroom. (Bachelard 1971:15, 177)

14. Figure of an otherworld woman wearing a guitar necklace, blouse, and painted-on Baule wrapper (close-up of illustration 11). Tiébissou region, Côte d'Ivoire, 1982. Photograph by Lap Nguyen Tien.

The statuary representation of the otherworld mate, in all its physicality and manipulability, constantly creates for its Baule possessor a powerfully affective reality that is not easy for the cultural outsider to appreciate fully. This was brought home to me in an interview I conducted with the carver Koffi Nianmien. Eighty-two years old at the time and still an active carver, he said in response to a question about his relationship to his *blolo bla* (ill. 15): "I

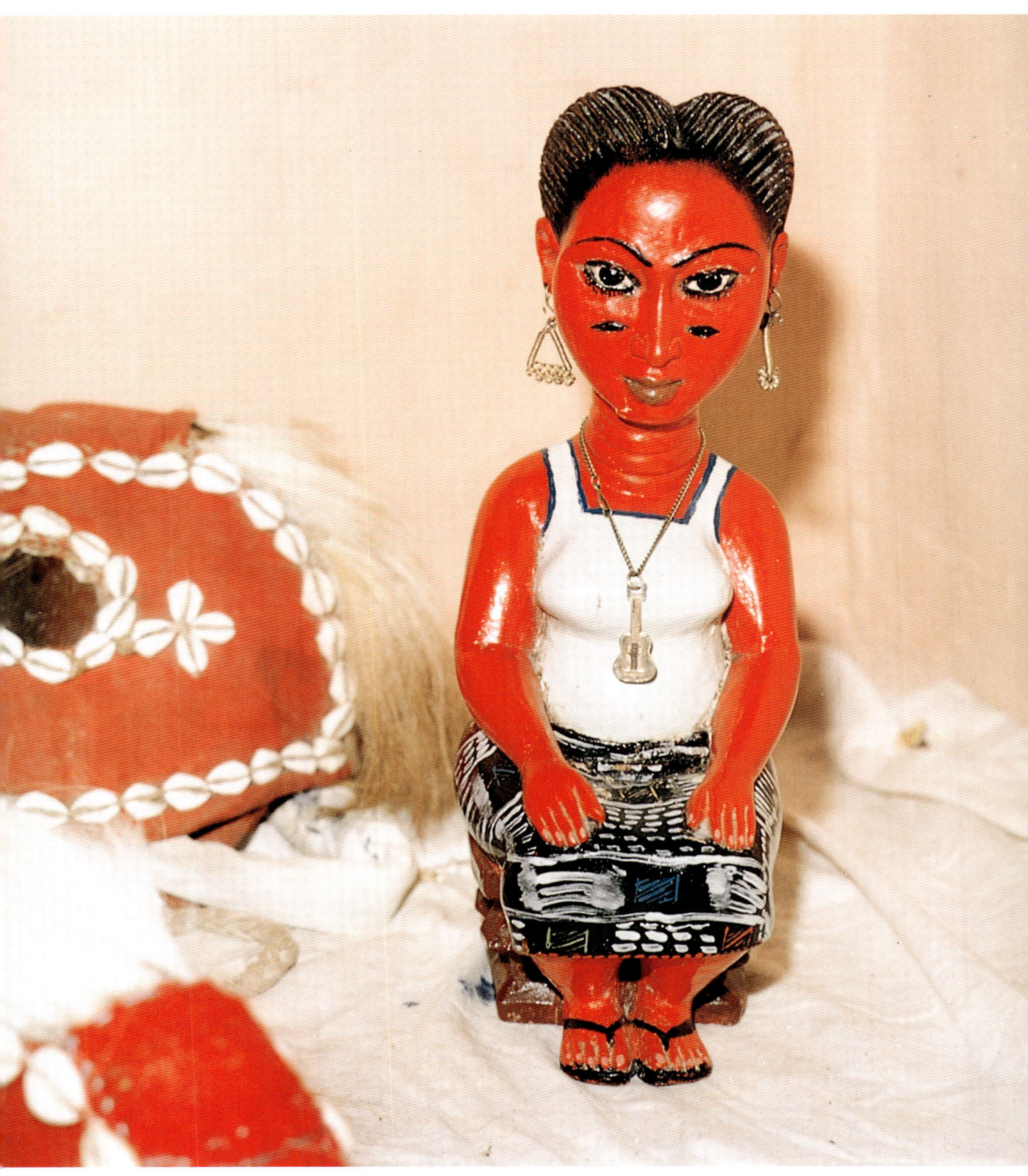

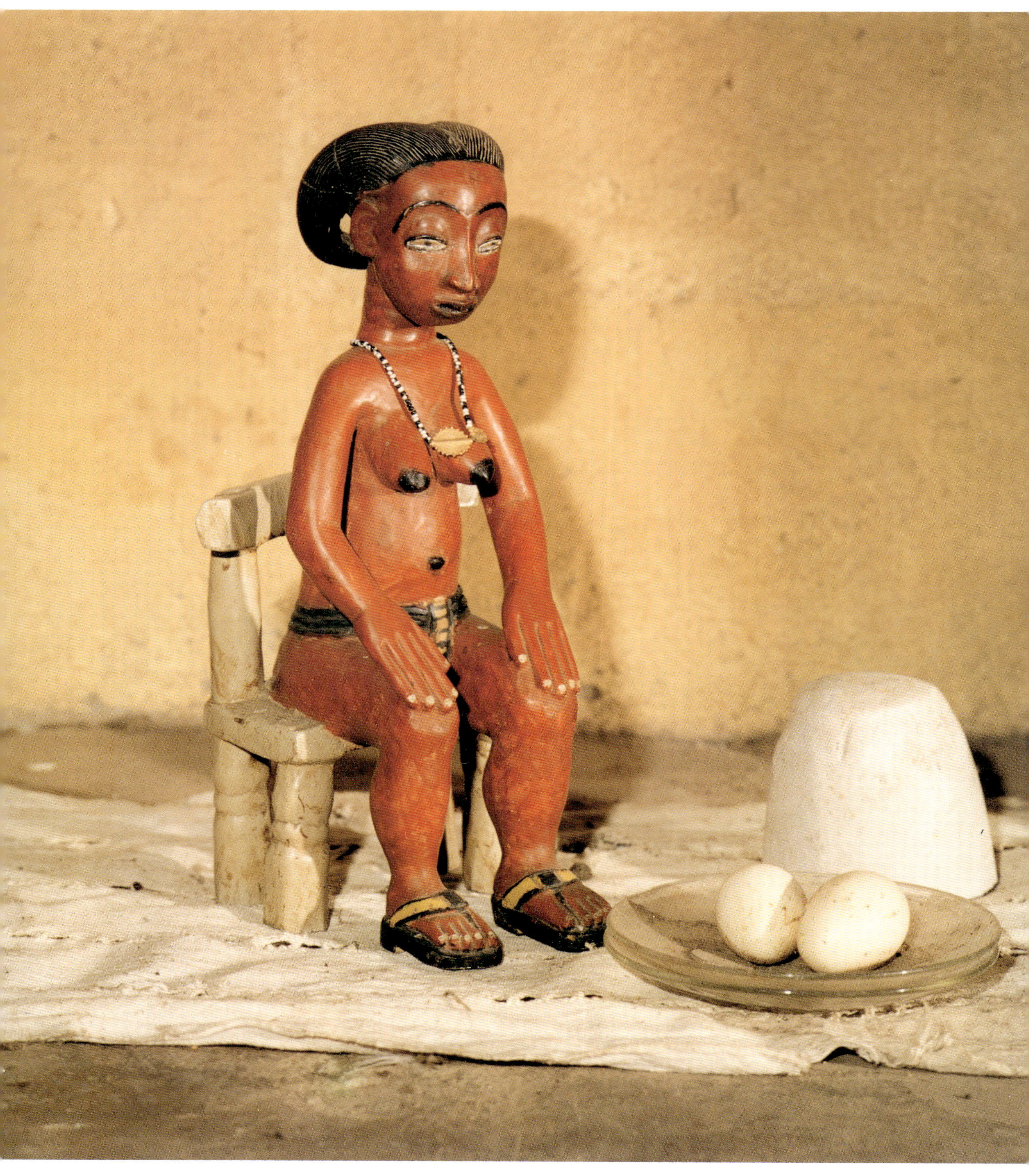

devote two days of the week to her. On Wednesdays I sleep alone. Sunday, I sleep alone too. On those days, I eat alone and I take care of her. If I need to offer her food, it is on those days." His face alight with joy and holding her image in his hands, he spoke of the woman with whom he had been intimately involved for more than fifty years. Widowed in the real world, his relationship with his otherworld woman continued to bring him pleasure.

The activeness of reverie interests me. I empathize with Bachelard's poetic interpretation of the night dream, which "does not belong to us. It is not our possession. With regard to us, it is an abductor, the most disconcerting of our abductors: it abducts our being from us" (1971:145). Remembered dreams and musings on the other-woman or other-man must have a profound effect on one's very being. Let us not forget that the *blolo* is an ideal world. Far off, accessible in dreams, inhabited principally by one unique person of the opposite sex, the otherworld must provide through reverie a place of repose. As Bachelard has stated: "[R]everie is a consciousness of well-being. In a cosmic image as well as in an image of our dwelling, we are in the well-being of repose" (pp. 177–78). The dreamer of reverie "can formulate a *cogito* at the center of his dreaming self" (p. 150). The dreamer of reverie is actively present in his or her reverie.

GENDER AND THE OTHERWORLD

In exploring the individual reality of the dreamworld as it is personified and transformed in art, and re-created in reverie, one has to deal with issues of gender, both in terms of its social constitution and, then, in its differential representation in art. It is not sufficient to assume that there is a basic equivalence in the psychological realities of the otherworld partner for a man and a woman. I have followed the lead of Pierre Étienne, the late French ethnographer of the Baule, in arguing that there is a fundamental dissymetry in Baule ideas about the respective attributes and characters of otherworld men and women. As discussed in chapter 1, women in the real world, unlike men, can never at a single time have more than one legitimate marital or sexual liaison.

15. Figure of an otherworld woman belonging to the sculptor Koffi Nianmien, with clay mound and egg offerings. Tiébissou region, Côte d'Ivoire, 1982. Photograph by Lap Nguyen Tien.

This difference in respective roles—the alternative mate for women versus the additional mate for men—allows for an appreciation of the *consciously* felt experiences that differentiate male and female attitudes to the other-mate in the *blolo*. As in other African societies, Baule custom has established a certain parity in co-wives' rights, particularly those of the conjugal bed; a man must be equitable in the nights he spends with each of his wives. In his schedule, the night reserved for his otherworld woman is factored in. His situation is significantly different, however, from the alternating cycle of a woman, who is visited by *either* her husband or her otherworld man.

The physical representation of a woman's otherworld man is also necessarily *other*—contrastive to both the physical and social attributes of her real-world husband. The artist's goal of idealizing human beauty in sculpture—a socially defined aspect of the canonical aesthetic—is already a testimony to the cultural determination of human aesthetics versus the physical definition of a human body: what *should* be versus what is. When, furthermore, the perfectly handsome otherworld man is depicted with the trappings of power, success, and status derived from the wider world, then the contrast becomes all the more acute. Over the past sixty years or so, Baule statues of otherworld men have been increasingly depicted with the clothes of Ivorian urban fashion. The traditionally nude male figure has to a very large degree been replaced by the contemporary clothed body, and the depiction of braided hairstyles has yielded to the representation of pith helmets, military headgear, hats, and barbershop haircuts.

If a woman's real-world husband is a modest peasant farmer, then the vision of her otherworld man as a successful city dweller provides her with a compelling, alternate reality. To the question as to what degree compensation plays a part in the female projection of this otherworld imagery, one can only speculate. At present there are simply not enough case studies on record for us to deal in depth with actual individual psychologies. Nonetheless I am convinced, on the basis of weekly observation of the Ivorian art trade over a period of fifteen years, that in the past few decades it has become as rare for a male statuette to be unclothed as it has been for a female figure to be clothed. There are, of course, exceptions (such as the minstrel's figure, ill. 12), but I would argue that such exceptions do not disprove the general rule. We are thus left with the question of the *why* of unclothed female figures.

If one accepts the wisdom of the common view that many African figurative sculptures function to localize and thereby control problematic spirits, with the corollary that their forms are therefore represented as human, then one is tempted to see the clothing depicted on Baule figures as a further attempt to personify and humanize in physical form a nonphysical being. The manner of the personification of Baule otherworld beings appears to be gender related: the depiction of a man's otherworld woman depends more on physical attributes of identity; the depiction of a woman's otherworld man relies more on the social dimensions of identity. But beyond this undoubtedly inadequate attempt at building a social or cultural explanatory model lies the psychological reality of individual experience, and especially the experience of art.

INDIVIDUAL EXPERIENCE AND ART

David Freedberg, in *The Power of Images: Studies in the History and Theory of Response* (1989:20–21), takes as his task "to consider why images elicit, provoke, or arouse the responses they do." He deals with a series of issues that relate to the efficacy of images, and although his focus of concern is largely European art history, his arguments and questions are also profoundly relevant for African art. Concerning the topic of consecration, he states that "it does seem to be the act of consecration that invests the image with the properties and powers that are either intended for it or subsequently attributed to it" (p. 84).

For the genre of Baule figurative art that we are discussing, consecration is the act that transforms the artist's work, the *waka sran* or statuette that actualizes the cultural canon, into an efficacious intermediary: the individual *blolo* image. No longer just a mere carving illustrative of its genre, it is personalized and activated for an individual as the effective and affecting image of his or her otherworld mate. The installation or lodging (*sike*) of the statuette is a performative act that formally announces and effectively brings into being a new state of affairs: previously ignored and neglected, and thus problematic, the otherworld partner is now officially greeted, recognized, and honored.[3] The statuette becomes something else—shall we call it art?—as it is transformed from the artist's carving to an individualized image representing a specific otherworld mate. It becomes capable of transformation, of *doing* things. The otherworld person is no longer an abstraction; he or she is now physically present, regularly addressed, handled, caressed, and fed, and the effect of the image is felt in the real-world arena of marital dynamics.

Freedberg's concern is to examine the power of objects. Why do works of art have a power that goes beyond that of words? What is the "precise role of figuration" in making objects effective? Going beyond the mere description of images, can one delve into the "relations between how they look and how they work?" (1989:135). To understand, if only in part, the power of *blolo* images, one must first appreciate the (socially constructed) fact that the *blolo* is a world that is exactly parallel to the real world of flesh and blood insofar as its inhabitants are perceived, experienced, and judged by the same standards of personhood and beauty as humans. *Blolo* images ideally represent the ultimate in human aesthetics. The epitome of human beauty is seen in finely sculpted faces, exquisitely detailed coiffures, elegantly long necks, well-developed chests, gently swelling bellies, beautifying scarification, potentially expressive pelvic circles, well-muscled hips and thighs, and strong calves (Vogel 1980). These cultural standards of beauty yield a certain comparability within the genre, but they are really only the backdrop against which the artist depicts and, most important, his client recognizes individuality in the *blolo* image. Freedberg's words about images of the Virgin, Christ, and the saints apply with equal relevance to *blolo* images. "Even if these images are considered the adequate mediators between people and what the images represent, they are always highly specified and differentiated mediators: as if their power resided wholly in their visual particularity" (1989:120). The visual particularity of a Baule *blolo* figure relates directly to the named individual it represents. The *blolo* is peopled with individuals, not families. One's relationship to a *blolo* partner is specific and dyadic; it constitutes two individuals linked together in a male-female sexual relationship, not two families linked together by the conventions and legal obligations of a socially recognized marriage. The unique individual who is the named *blolo* partner is represented by what is intended to be, and always perceived as, a highly specific image. Facial beauty, coiffure, musculature, stance, skin color, scarification, clothing, and accoutrements all combine to both define and concretize the specific identity of the dreamed partner from the *blolo*. To look at the *blolo* image is to imagine the *blolo* mate. The image becomes the prop of reverie.

TIME, PLACE, AND REPRESENTATION

I have discussed various ideas about the representation of the individual *blolo* mate, but still remain unsatisfied with the larger issue of the "artness" of these images. What is it in them and in the culture in which they are created that defines or qualifies them as art? What makes them capable of provoking response? What makes them capable of *doing?* Gregory Bateson's brilliant essay "Style, Grace, and Information in Primitive Art" (1973) provides us with an interesting framework for another attempt at cross-cultural looking.

> That aspect of the work of art which can most easily be reduced to words—the *mythology* connected with the subject matter—is not what I want to discuss. . . . To translate the art object into mythology and then examine the mythology would only be a neat way of dodging or negating the problem of "what is art?" (P. 236)

Bateson's concern is with "what important psychic information is in the art object quite apart from what it may 'represent.'" Rightfully he points us to larger issues of "the complex layering of consciousness and unconsciousness . . . that creates difficulty when we try to discuss art or ritual or mythology" (p. 240). His ideas are appealing, especially in his formulation of the idea that "art becomes . . . an exercise in communicating about the species of the unconscious" (p. 242).

The mythologies connected with *blolo* imagery are conscious and can be articulated. They can be discussed and investigated through the kind of cultural exegesis that we have dealt with so far. Other aspects of this culturally created art genre probably cannot be articulated, especially in relation to the specific *blolo* image, for the very power of the object lies in the fact that it cannot be translated into words. "Art represents an expressive necessity that places itself *outside of* ('beyond' and 'before') language. Not only are 'art objects' mute, but they are not made superfluous by *signs* (of any kind, including words)" (Pellizzi 1990–91:5). The answer to the question of the "artness" of *blolo* imagery is thus not necessarily to be found in more fieldwork or more insightful comments from those who create, use, and regard the art. In fact, the answer *per se* is unattainable. I do, however, as a human being concerned with existential questions of meaning, muse on the artfulness of the *blolo* figure as a solution to the angst-filled question *why* that is uttered by the human soul in times of crisis.

The crises that ultimately lead to the creation of *blolo* images are profound crises of human existence, of identity and meaning. They are provoked by inescapable failure, whether it be the failure to conceive, to marry, to establish an ongoing relationship, to bring forth living children, to be successful as defined by others and by oneself. In this, the all-too-real world of personal inadequacy experienced in life lived in groups, what existential or psychological space is created by the belief in, the experienced and conscious knowledge of, the *blolo?* I am not referring here to the shared cultural belief of the Baule in the existence of another world, the *blolo.* I am, rather, talking about the individual who specifically creates and experiences that place for himself or herself. No longer a received notion or a socially determined abstraction, the *blolo* suddenly becomes immanently and individually real because of the recognition of a single and unique person who exists outside of time and outside of place, and who exists, furthermore, uniquely and unrelentingly in a permanently pervading relationship to oneself.

The individual who incorporates the *blolo* into his or her life can purposefully step out of time, for the *blolo* both precedes and will succeed time as it is normally experienced. The soul of the newborn comes from there, and the soul of the departed goes there; yet any notion of linear time, chronology, or teleology that would seem to be implied in these ideas has to be contrasted with the otherness of the *blolo* as experienced. The *blolo* is the ultimate other, the fruit of a cosmic reverie, which "possesses a sort of stability and tranquility. It helps us escape time. It is a *state.* Let us get to the bottom of its essence: it is a state of mind. . . . The soul does not live on the edge of time. It finds its rest in the universe imagined by reverie" (Bachelard 1971:14–15).

Andrew Benjamin's reflections on spacing and distancing (1991) are particularly relevant to my own musings on the timeless "thereness" of the *blolo* (*lo,* with its insistence on "there") for the Baule. He asks, "What then is the experience of distance?" and subsequently states that "distance comes to be experienced as always involving *the ineliminable presence of an otherness* that can never be overcome in the struggle for synthesis" (pp. 44, 45; emphasis added). He later argues that

> between any two "points" not only will there be distance, there will also be a relation. Distance and relation are to that extent inter-articulated. One does not precede the other. The mode of being proper to this relation is complex. A relation will always involve distancing and spacing. It is however only if the held-apart is taken as held-apart that relation emerges as central. (P. 57)

This holding apart, according to Benjamin, yields an "anoriginal," or "primordial," presence: the "primordially present held-apart" (p. 58).

The primordial timelessness or immutability of the *blolo* image that focuses on youth, whether male or female, has a particular type of appeal—an appeal that is not minor, evoking as it does all the power of sexual exploration and knowledge gained at the peak of youthful sexuality. I would further argue that this appeal is significantly reinforced by a corollary appeal: that of privacy. As opposed to the *here* of other people, problems, and changefulness, there exists (fortunately) a *there* (the *lo* of *blolo*), which, through an individual's *blolo* mate, defines but the individual. This private reality is mutually affirming: it defines one, and one defines it. One's private, individual existence defined by the *blolo* is further confirmed by the physical reality of the created work of art. And paradoxically the state of privacy also assumes a public face; it becomes a fact recognized by others, especially one's spouse. The art, that is, the individual and individualized image of the other-being, makes evident, in all its complexity, a radically different world—different in terms of place, of time, and (perhaps most important) of gender. *This* reality is now countered by *that* reality: "Relation is important within aesthetics because its centrality will yield an approach to the object that does not take the relation between subject and object as a totality but as the interplay of identity and difference; of same and other. This generates a different object" (Benjamin 1991:58–59). The work of art embodies the longing—and hope—for that which may be unattainable. Art, again to quote Bateson, "is part of man's quest for grace; sometimes his ecstasy in partial success, sometimes his rage and agony at failure" (1973:239).

Thus we can think of Baule figurative art. The *blolo* image evokes a primordial otherness; it speaks of a held-apart space that is experienced individually and that is immutably different from the reality of the present moment. It simultaneously stresses and minimizes distance. And it paradoxically embodies and accentuates the apartness and otherness of the *blolo* while materially representing it as a living presence. The work of art "gives presence to what had hitherto not been presented" (Benjamin 1991:61). The goal is not to synthesize differing realities; it is, rather, to hold apart another place and thus to affirm the constancy of its other reality. The appeal to this primordial, timeless, and spatially defined difference makes possible reverie and, as a consequence, reflection on the lived experience. If other realities exist, then perhaps one *can* escape the constraints of current reality and affirm the potential for things, and personal existence, to be otherwise.

Chapter Four

SEXUALITY, DESIRE, AND VERISIMILITUDE

In the imagined world of the *blolo,* made up of isolated individuals, how does sexuality affect the representation of the male and female in art? Beyond individual yearnings, what is the cultural psychology of desire? How is realism or verisimilitude conveyed in the work of art? Let us turn again to Freedberg (1989:317) and his discussion "Arousal by Image." In a series of provocative questions, he asks:

> What if every conscious act of looking were part of the intentionality of desire? And if the desire to gaze on representation were like the desire to gaze on the object; and the drive to do so, in the West at least, were masculine? What then would be the implications for the investigator of response?

SEXUALITY AND REPRESENTATION

Bearing in mind the contemporary tendency for *blolo* images of men to be clothed and those of women to be unclothed, we must now deal with "the general representation of female bodies in ways that meet male standards of eroticism" (Freedberg 1989:322). Female *blolo* images are most often totally nude. Not only are breasts, subtly swelling bellies, and hip lines (*bo nenglen*) depicted with finesse, the external female sexual organs are often also quite accurately represented. Female statues make visually accessible the part of the female anatomy that is otherwise held to be the most powerful fetish of all, a thing that when seen by a man can kill (Guerry 1972:45).[1] This part of the figure is usually covered with a miniature *cache-sexe,*[2] but nonetheless *in private* (a notion to which we shall return) the most secret part of the female anatomy can be made accessible for viewing (ill. 17).

The fact that in the past both male and female statuettes were carved with clearly depicted genitalia is significant for our discussion of consecration, the ceremony in which the *blolo* partner is informed that a statuary stand-in has been created and henceforth will receive offerings on his or her behalf. It was in preparation for this ceremony that the *cache-sexe* and the beads or string

16. Figure of an otherworld man with a sharply parted hairstyle, facial scarification, and neck lines, and wearing a shirt, elastic-waisted shorts, wristwatch, beaded bracelet, and sandals, c. 1965, height 33.5 cm. Fowler Museum of Cultural History, University of California, Los Angeles, X94.18.1.

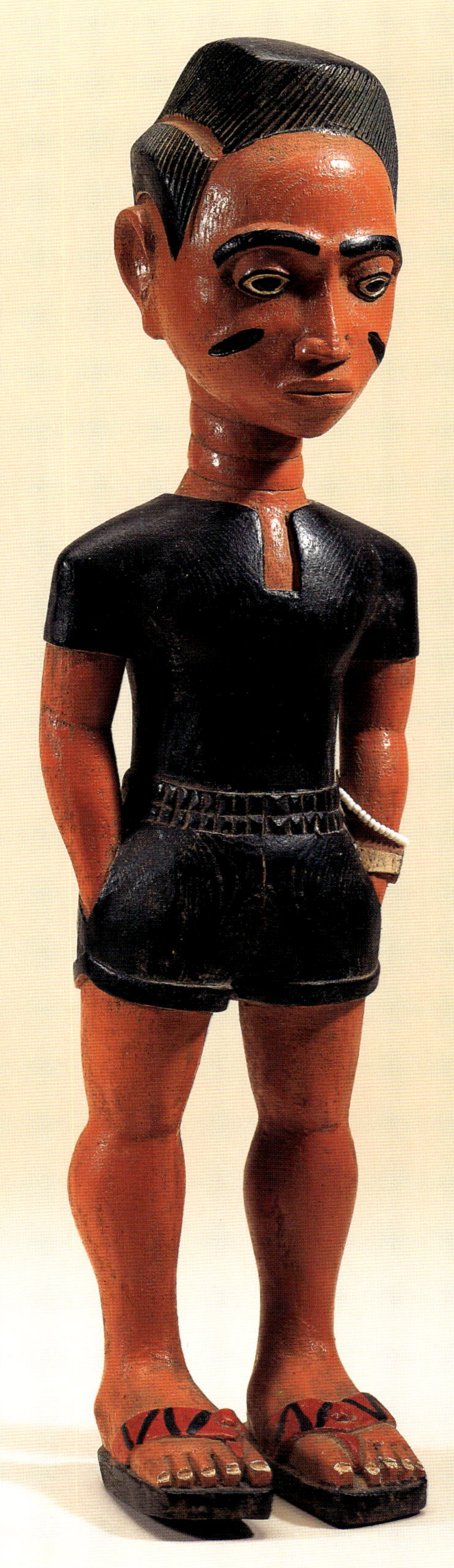

that support it (and at the same time emphasize the pelvic circle, or *bo nɛn-glen*) were added to the carved figure by its owner. This action was a critical moment in the transformation of the figure from a sculpted statuette, *waka sran,* into the efficacious, particularized *blolo* image, now properly lodged in its owner's home.[3] The recourse to the completion of the work of art by the use of an actual piece of cloth as a *cache-sexe* is of particular significance. Freedberg, in his discussion of Juan Martínez Montañés's *Jesus de la Pasión* (ca. 1615–1618), a figure covered in an actual robe bound with a knotted and tasseled cord, says that "it is not as if Montañés were unable to carve a robe that gave the illusion of reality" but that the "recourse to real garments . . . demonstrates, finally, the insistent impulse to merge living qualities with inert substance" (1989:245). According to his argument, the images he writes about "were intended to be as realistic as possible" and "capable of being perceived as living presence."

The covering of the genitalia of the *blolo* figure with cloth imposes cultural order on the most troublesome component of the figure's sexuality. The figure becomes more human—more of a person (*sran*)[4]—by the imposition of a socially constructed modesty. In terms of its consecration, the figure is dressed in this way *before* it is greeted, lodged, and fed. The use of a real (albeit miniature) *cache-sexe,* which accentuates the primary sexual areas, augments the figure's lifelikeness and natural sexuality—a primal, powerful force—making it a more effective "living presence." It must be admitted, however, that "[i]n concealing nature, the cover, of course, makes nature all the more titillating. The cover invites exposure; it always bears the potential of striptease" (Stewart 1984:114). Thus the cloth *cache-sexe* may actually increase the erotic appeal of the figure; in art, as in life, the partially clothed figure may indeed be more erotic than the "wholly undraped and unadorned female figure" (Lucie-Smith 1991:178).

The apparently contradictory impulses of both representation (in wood) and repression (through cloth) of the primary sexual organs of the other-world mate mirror the ambiguities of human sexuality, especially female sexuality. It is believed that the female genitalia can cause death when seen by the male gaze, and yet can also unleash a primordial power that can be socially redemptive, as when women encircle their village at night and drop their *caches-sexe* at the intersection of paths in order to protect a village from impending calamity (Guerry 1972:45; Étienne 1976:32 n. 15).[5]

The representation of male and female in art must be understood in terms of basic Baule ideas about sexual relations and marriage, notably the emphasis on a young woman's need to demonstrate her fecundity *prior* to marriage. The onset of menstruation is recognized in different ways in different parts of the Baule region; in the northern central region of the Aari and Faafouè,

17. Figure of an other-world woman wearing a cotton *cache-sexe* supported by hip beads, c. 1920, height 31 cm. Fowler Museum of Cultural History, University of California, Los Angeles, X94.77.12.

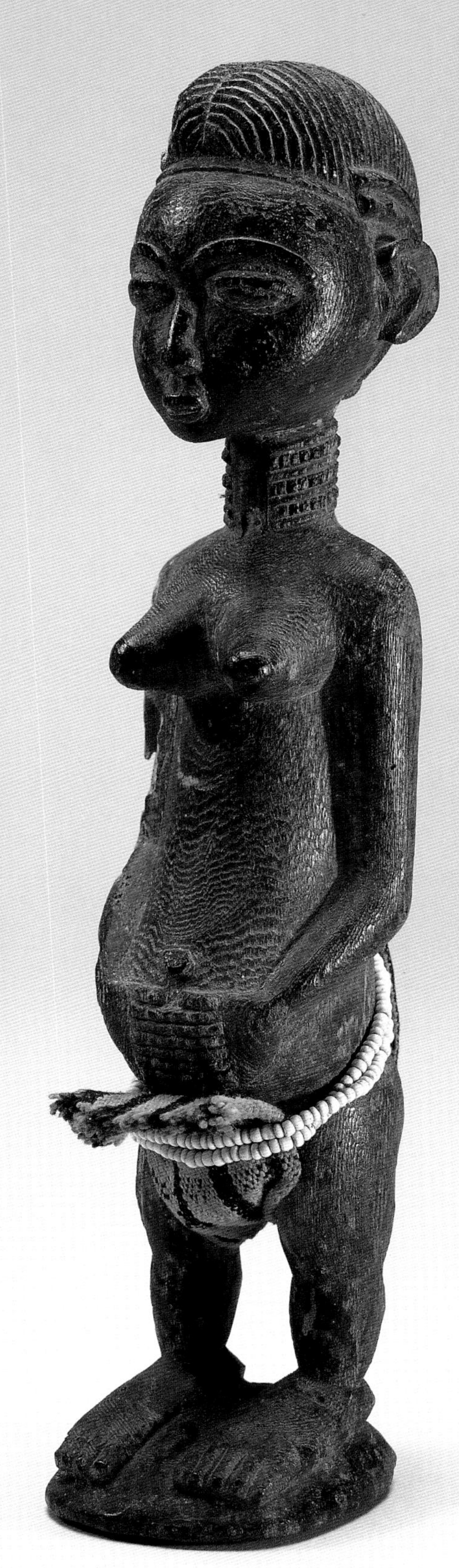

whose cultural practices are described by Father Vincent Guerry, the new status of a girl after her first menstruation is recognized by the older women of the family, who at dawn

> enter the girl's bedroom, and wake her by hitting her with a white *cache-sexe*. They say to her, "Here is the *cache-sexe* which we are giving you; you are [now] grown-up, if you have a child, it will be a child of our house." Henceforth, she is available to her courters, not for a proper marriage—it is too early—but so that she may bring forth children; that is what is important. (Guerry 1972:41–42)

The offering of the *cache-sexe* (more ample and more covering than the one that the young girl wore before) is a cultural recognition of her potential for childbearing and an act whose "first goal is to legitimize the child" that she will bear. Thus the *cache-sexe* symbolizes in a very real way her adult sexuality and procreative powers. The waistband beads that support it also have erotic potential. The experienced eroticism of real life has a direct resonance in the *real* beads and *cache-sexe* around the pelvic circle of the sculpted female figure. We can agree with John Berger's argument that the "nude is always conventionalized—and the authority for its conventions derives from a certain tradition of art" and that, furthermore, "it is quite clear that the nude also relates to lived sexuality" (1972:53).

In *blolo* images the most visually prominent aspects of the female anatomy pertaining to sexuality are the breasts (see ills. 1, 17, 18). It can be argued that the conventional Baule depiction of female breasts in art is one that stresses potentiality—the potentiality of procreation and motherhood. In other words, from the male point of view, breasts may well evoke the potency of possession and impregnation. Here it is worth quoting Freedberg.

> [I]t would be futile wholly to argue away the psychosexual dimension of the bare female breast in all cultures, or of the exposed genitalia, male or female. The exact limits of the resonance of the breast in the psychopathology of everyday life may vary from one culture to another, but the limits are only somewhat variable, certainly not so much that they never intersect. (1989:324)

18. Figure of an other-world woman with a tressed hairstyle and neck lines, and a *cache-sexe* with hip beads, c. 1925, height 31.5 cm. Fowler Museum of Cultural History, University of California, Los Angeles, X94.62.6.

In *blolo* images, breasts are the defining feature of the trunk (*afien*), which is usually not further differentiated into chest and belly. Breasts and belly form a composite for both psychosexually affective and sculptural considerations.

The breasts of potentiality are clearly those of a maiden (*talua*), a female who is moving from girlhood to womanhood and is enjoying her youth. The Baule cultural expectation for a young person is that he or she will fully enjoy the new bloom of physical maturity prior to marriage and the obligations of adult life. This is the age at which young people preen themselves to be seen

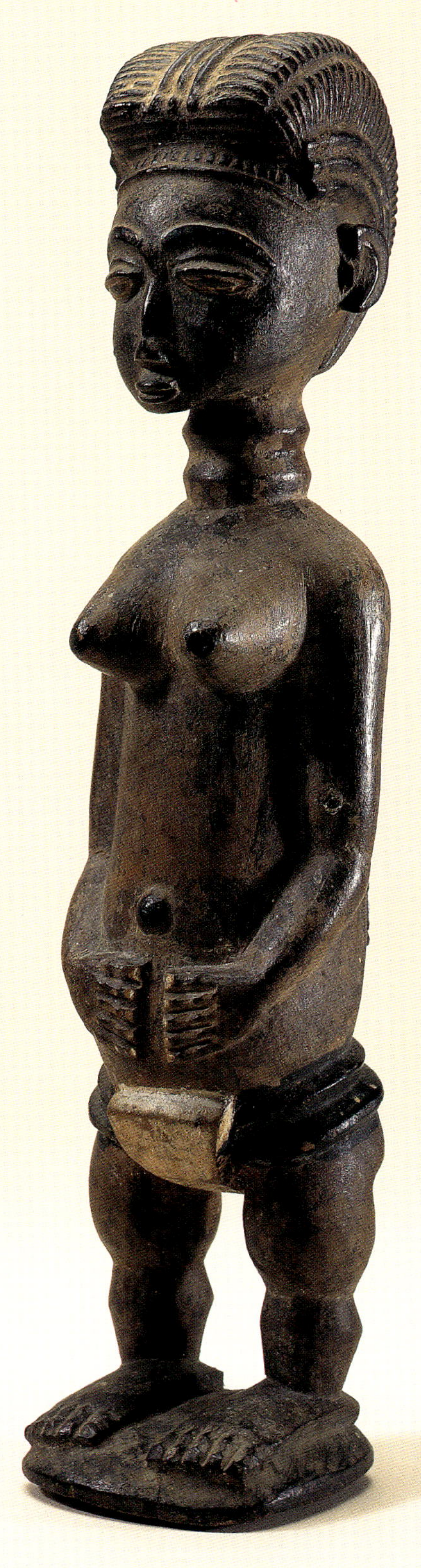

by their peers. In former times young people beautified their bodies through scarification; nowadays they bring clothes into play in the presentation of self. No wonder then that the word *gbaflen* (young man) is synonymous with dandy.

A maiden's breasts are a sign of not-too-distant motherhood, the physical markers of her new sexual potential. The breasts of a statuette, however, are timeless—continually attractive and always available. They will never nurse a baby, and they will never sag. For the Baule, one of the immediate effects of childbirth is that sexual relations between man and wife cease until the child is weaned. The nursed breast is therefore a signal of sexual nonavailability, or marital nonaccessibility. Infrequently one finds depicted in art an otherworld woman who either carries or holds a baby, even sometimes to her breast. This would seem to argue against an interpretation of the female figure as a representation of timelessness. Yet the depiction of a nursing mother or even the depiction of a bearded, and thus older, man is also an image of stasis, a steady state unaffected by time. An image of achievement, whether that of childbirth or of age, can be as much a statement of timelessness as the image of potential found in the female breast.

> [T]he ideal of the body exists within an illusion of stasis, an illusion that the body does not change and that those conditions and contingencies which shape the ideal are transcendent and "classic" as well. Between the here-and-now of lived experience and this ideal is a distance which creates and maintains desire. (Stewart 1984:116)

The stasis of the ideal body also holds true for the representation of the male body in *blolo* images. As discussed in chapter 1, a young man's pectoral muscles indicate social character and his likely success as a farmer. Indeed, in a male figure the tension and prominence of the pectoral muscles are the principal features that create his male identity. He, too, is a timeless ideal, usually an ideal of physical strength. Male figures, however, often incorporate features that indicate relative age; this is especially the case with bearded figures, for the beard (restricted in real life to older men) indicates both age and the increase in respect and social standing accorded to those senior to oneself (ill. 19). The sexuality of male and female figures is represented and perceived quite differently partly, I believe, because all figures are carved by male artists.

THE ARTIST AND THE MALE IMAGINATION

19. Figure of an otherworld man with a beard, c. 1900, height 45 cm. Private collection. Photograph by Denis Nervig.

Earlier I posed the question of why individuals might commission images with particular characteristics—females asking for socially successful males, males asking for physically potent females. We may also ask whether the answer to this puzzle might be found in the artist as much as in the client who commissions and uses the image.[6] Could the artist be the principal agent,

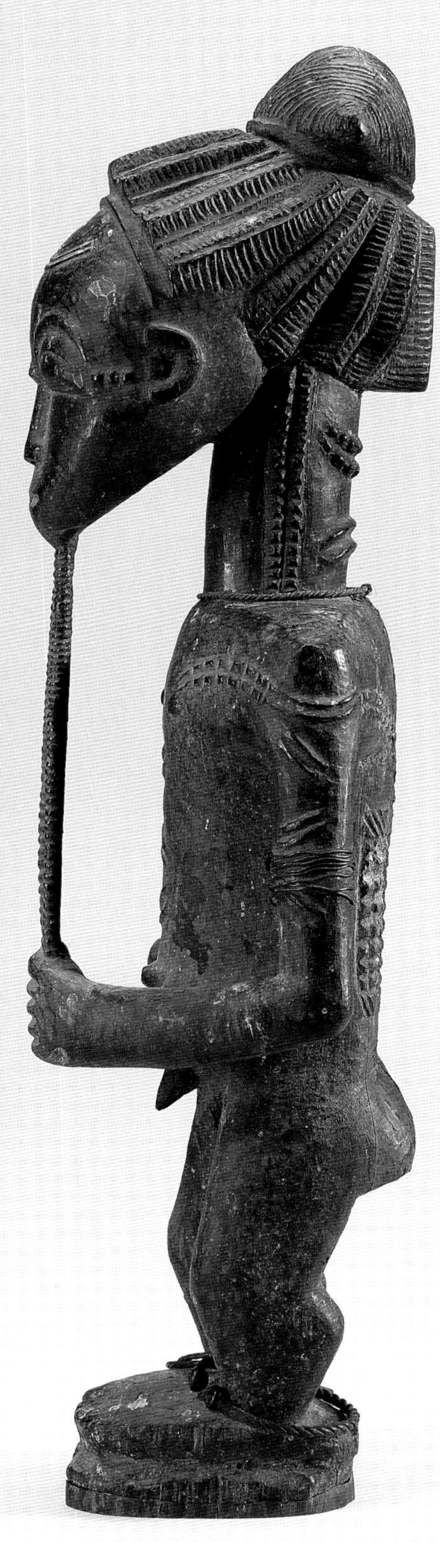

the prime mover, who creates both the image of the ideal female, stressing her physicality, *and* the image of the ideal male, stressing his sociocultural status? Is the Baule artist the reflexive questioner and interpreter of what otherwise is, or could be? To begin to think about the artist, let me quote, and extrapolate from, some ideas put forth by Wendy Lesser in *His Other Half: Men Looking at Women through Art.*

> A male artist who thinks about that purely potential other existence—the self he might have been, the unborn sister he replaced [or the ideal sexual partner in another world]—will also be thinking about determinism, and the possible ways around it. Art offers ways to break the cycle of determinism, to win a second chance at getting things right. (1991:265)

The Baule sculptor thinks about that "purely potential other existence" in a different way. He does not work from a live model to create his sculpture; rather, he works from an active mind. His task is not the interpretation or abstraction of a figure standing in front of his eyes; it is the *imagination* of an unseen person and the concentration of that person's essence in material form. He strives for human and individual resemblance in his work; he strives to create verisimilitude, a living presence.

Liam Hudson and Bernardine Jacot, in their work on the male imagination (1991), argue that "men may be distinguished in the arts by their need to produce works which have their point of origin in sexual desire" (p. 139). They discuss the idea that men's gratification in sexual intimacy may cause them to "'petrify' the women in their lives" by turning them into works of art (p. 141). They further assert that "while few may achieve it, the ambition to remove the object of desire from time and space in this way—to transfix or eternalise it—is widespread; and it is the gratification of this urge that, in turn, furnishes our culture with many of its most compelling icons and texts." In the implicit model of the Western artist standing before his subject, there is a presumed artistic trajectory that moves from the immediacy of *here* (or her) to the removed *there* of the work of art. For the Baule sculptor, however, the trajectory is different: from a preexistent there (the *lo,* or "thereness," of the *blolo*) he transfixes (*jra,* "brings down") with his adze an imagined presence, so that *here* it is "the imprisonment of presence" in his representation that "gives the fixed image its potentiality" (Freedberg 1989:234).

In my interview with the sculptor Koffi Nianmien, I asked him provocatively whether he had himself carved the statue of his *blolo bla.* His disdainful response was a rhetorical question: "Does one sleep with one's own daughter?" His reply not only affirmed the palpable sexuality of the female figure he so lovingly cared for and caressed; it also confirmed the implicit Baule attitude that to carve figures is to engage in an act of procreation. For Nianmien the figures he carved were in a very real sense his sons and daughters. *His* figure of his otherworld mate thus necessarily had to be the "daughter" of another sculptor. Clearly, the sexuality of the living presence he held in his hands had to be other than the work of his own hands.

The Baule sculptor, in sculpting a figure that represents a *blolo* mate, seeks to create an object of desire not for himself but for someone else. The solitary artist of Western art traditions contemplates his model to create an image for a future spectator. The Baule sculptor, however, is challenged to create an image on the basis of a verbal description of her (or his) form and attributes furnished by his client, the future spectator. There thus arises an interesting complicity between artist and client that leads to the creation of an object of desire; they join in a common imagining. Should the artist *also* dream of the otherworld person that he is to represent, the complicity thickens; the otherworld person participates in the collusion by offering him access to the heretofore restricted privacy of her (or his) presence.

All Baule sculptors are male. This socially constituted fact must be acknowledged if we are to reflect upon the artist and the male imagination. Although, as Abigail Solomon-Godeau points out, "there is little need to underscore the fact that, historically, women have rarely been the authors of their own representations, either as makers or models" (1993:273). For the male artist, the female is always *other;* the male is always, even if only to a limited degree, *self*. The frameworks for the conceptual imagination and idealization of female and male are opposed. The Baule male artist responding to the male client and agreeing to create an image of this distant, otherworld woman, is in a different existential position than when he responds to a female client and agrees to create her otherworld man. The artist thinks about each differently as he conceives them and as he looks at each in the process of creation. Both the work-in-creation and the created work confront the artist differently. His experience in carving female breasts *must* be different from his experience in carving a male chest, and the same must hold true, but with an even greater intensity of felt difference, as he depicts the primary sexual organs. His male gaze sees male and female differently as he brings each into being.

Thinking about the lack of a live model in the Baule practice of sculpture is to consider—to imagine—the series of images, half-images, and details that the artist must draw upon as he thinks the figurative object into being. "The poetry of bare flesh as an artistic subject induces every sculptor to become, after a fashion, a painter, and arouses in him a taste for the warmth of reality. Flesh becomes flesh; it loses the quality of stone" (Focillon 1992:57). The pictures of the mind's eye are images drawn from his experience, from the stock of refracted impressions the artist has constructed as he has repeatedly examined the difference of form found in the nubility of a young maiden or the developing musculature of a youth. The young woman may remind him of the yearnings of his own adolescence; the young man may remind him of his own transition from youth to man. When he concentrates on the form of the female body, he probably draws more upon his mental images of young women than older women, for their form is more revealed, their breasts not yet covered by the wrapped cloth (*tanni*) used to carry a child on the back. The form of the male figure he creates, too, is probably inspired by his nostalgic perception of the taut muscles and virility of young adulthood. The realism of female and male figures comes from his imaginings of what was and what, through his hands, will be.

ART AND THE IMAGINED WORLD

Kendall Walton proposes that "representational works of art generally are props in games of make-believe" (1990:51). He states that "the role of props in generating fictional truths is enormously important. They give fictional worlds and their contents a kind of objectivity, an independence from cognizers and their experiences which contributes much to the excitement of our adventures with them" (p. 42). He goes on to argue that the "excitement of exploring the unknown will be lost to the extent that we explore the worlds ourselves. But if we let others (artists) construct them for us, we can enjoy not only the excitement but also the benefits of any special talent and insight they might bring to the task" (pp. 67–68). Inherent in the Baule notion of the existence of the *blolo* is an idea that *that* world is a world one chooses to believe in *even though* it is a place "which exists beyond sensory experience" (Étienne 1976:30). There is an agreement to agree on the existence of the *blolo* both at the level of the shared Baule worldview and at the level of individual experience and knowledge. The special role of the Baule artist is to reify the make-believe in a work of art. The revealed knowledge of divination is to be substantiated and corroborated by the form of art revealed through the special talent and insight of the male artist.

Divination for the Baule is above all a public event. Knowledge is not only revealed; it is made into public knowledge.[7] The *raison d'être* of a situation is made known by the diviner, and a collaborative consensus is thereby established between all parties. Everyone concerned "buys into" a common understanding. When divination reveals that a state of events is due to the intervention of the otherworld partner, then the private reality of dreams is socially validated as a parallel real reality. The un-reality of the distant otherworld (or, for the Baule, one should perhaps rather speak of the transcendent Ur-reality of the *blolo*) is countered by a tangible, immediate evidence: the realistic figure that represents the otherworld partner. He or she can now be held in one's hands, talked to, cared for, and contemplated. To others, especially one's spouse, the figure is also evidence of the existence of one's *blolo* partner.

The critical task of the sculptor is to create verisimilitude in the figure, the realism that allows the figure to stand as a living presence. Implicit in my thinking, of course, is a focus on those otherworld figures that are truly accomplished, well interpreted, carefully executed, and fully three-dimensional works of art. While many Baule sculpted figures are *not* complex works of art, some even being barely sufficient to represent a general human form, I choose to explore those that express individuality and convey personality, those that make it possible to imagine fully another being. And here it is important to resituate the object in its original context of appreciation. The complicity of artist and client having resulted in the creation of a particular form, a unique figure that has been duly consecrated, wherein now lies its appreciation?

THE FIGURE AS MINIATURE

Let us reflect on the *blolo* image's initial locus of appreciation by putting the figure back in the hands of its owner, its real-world mate. Let us think of it as literally in the hands, for its original apprehension as a representational image comes simultaneously through the visual and the sensual, the eye and the hand. It is framed and grasped by the hand, which is, in Susan Stewart's words, "the measure of the miniature" (1984:46).

In the twentieth century, Baule figures have tended to be about a foot or so in height, but we have not really reflected on the issue of scale, or the fact that the *blolo* image is in fact a miniature. Stewart, whose chapter "The Miniature" in *On Longing: Narratives of the Miniature, the Gigantic, the Souvenir, the Collection* (1984) has informed and influenced my reflections, asserts that "there are no miniatures in nature; the miniature is a cultural product, the product of an eye performing certain operations, manipulating, and attending in certain ways to, the physical world" (p. 54). She contends that

> the metaphoric world of the miniature makes everyday life absolutely anterior and exterior to itself. The reduction in scale which the miniature presents skews the time and space relations of the everyday lifeworld, and *as an object consumed, the miniature finds its "use value" transformed into the infinite time of reverie*. . . . [There is a] capacity of the miniature to create an "other" time, a type of transcendent time which negates change and the flux of lived reality. (P. 65; emphasis added)

It is the *blolo* figure, the miniature person (*sran*), that facilitates the daytime world of private reverie with its inversion in many ways of the private nighttime world of the dream. In the unconscious dream the *blolo* mate is the initiator, the agent who comes to one. In conscious reverie[8] one initiates one's own participation in the *blolo*, perhaps while holding or regarding the *blolo* image. It is to the handled, contemplated, and consumed image that we must turn our attention.

Let us think about the *blolo* figure through the perception, the cultural eye, of its original beholder.[9] What cultural presuppositions or propensities does he or she bring to the figure and its contemplation? How are perception and imagination informed by culturally specific ideas? What is seen and what is evoked by this or that component of the figure, or specific detail? What, in the material nature of the object, evokes the intentionality of desire within which reverie occurs?

One must begin this exploration with an appreciation of the "beingness" that inheres in the object. As a person in wood (*waka sran*), the figure makes it possible to believe in the existence of an otherworld mate with whom communication is possible. There is in all Baule figures the ambiguity of a fundamental composure or serenity—each is a poised being at rest—that serves to evoke a *living presence*. In the figure is a perceptible personification, an attribution of human nature or character. Whether or not one chooses to think of the figure as a portrait of the otherworld mate or simply as a figurative stand-in for that mate, the form makes possible a confident belief that another *person* truly exists in the *blolo*.

VERISIMILITUDE AND INDIVIDUAL PERSONHOOD IN IMAGES

For the owner the *blolo* image stands in for a *specific* otherworld person. The figure demonstrates certain features of Baule style[10] that can be discussed by the art historian in terms of presumed typicality, uniqueness, or idiosyncrasy, but within these overall parameters, every figure is unique in its specific form and consequent identity. Each figure is perceived individually. In the processes of carving and adornment of the figure, there is a "striving for verisimilitude . . . the striving toward reproduction of total reality" (Freedberg 1989:206). For the individual viewer, a "constitutive verisimilitude" is achieved, "a resemblance that re-produces." Held in the hand, the image reproduces the presence, and evokes the essence, of the *blolo* partner and in so doing activates reverie.

In the appreciation and interpretation of any *blolo* image, the importance of the sculptural interpretation of the face and head must be given due place, for it is above all in the face that personhood is represented and identity is found. The face of the image conveys a sense of individual being in the same way that in real life a person's face is the primary visual focus for his or her potential interlocutor. For example, the identification of a person in terms of the three skin tones recognized by the Baule—dark, light, red—is based on the tone of skin perceived on the forehead. Susan Vogel, discussing her field study of Baule aesthetics in which she showed a group of figures to Baule men, points out that the face was the most commented upon part of a figure, for "[c]ritics could hardly be indifferent to the head and face, and particularly the eyes of figures in a culture where these features show a person's intelligence, consciousness and presence" (1980:10).

In *blolo* figures, as in many other genres of African art, the head receives a greater proportional emphasis than any other part of the body, typically representing from one-fourth to one-third of the overall height of a figure. It is almost as though within the figure-as-miniature, the body is further miniaturized so as to form a pedestal, a supportive column, for the head; the body is a base for the neck, which in turn is a base for the head. Moreover, as the head is set off from the body, so, too, is the face carefully set off from the sculptural mass of the head. In carving the general volume of the head, the artist emphasizes the frontality of the figure through the face. The face is usually framed and established as a more or less oval shape within the line of the jaw, which meets the line that delimits the coiffure where it meets the forehead. The figure receives a focus through the face; the face receives its focus from the eyes, its dominant feature. A quotation from Alberto Giacometti is particularly apropos.

> One does want to sculpt a living person, but what makes him alive is without doubt his gaze. The heads from the New Hebrides are true, *are more than true,* because they have a gaze. Not the imitation of eyes, but really and truly a gaze. Everything else is only the framework for the gaze. . . . If the gaze, that is, life, is the main thing, then the head becomes the main thing . . . the rest of the body is limited to functioning as antennae that make people's life possible—the life that is housed in the skull. (Ashton 1985:57)

Indeed, so it is for the Baule: "Everything else is only the framework for the gaze." They would agree with Giacometti's conditional statement, "If the gaze, that is, life, is the main thing, then the head becomes the main thing."

It is in the implicitly volitional and "conscious" gaze that one perceives the otherworld mate as person. Eyes are the "ultimate measure of living presence" (Freedberg 1989:244). They "provide the most immediate testimony of life in living beings; in images . . . they are even more powerfully capable of doing so" (p. 202). For the Baule, the eyes are *the* critical metaphor for awareness and personhood. The metaphor of the gaze is constantly evoked, as in the following phrases: *i nyi wo su,* "his eyes are open" (he is alive); *i nyi a ti,* "his eyes have been opened" (he has reached the age of reason, or he is open to new ideas); *i nyi so mi,* "his eyes worship me" (he respects me). The gaze of a *blolo* figure signals consciousness, engaging the viewer and asserting a living and attentive presence. "The human face is above all a composite of the receptive organs" (Focillon 1992:158).

In the artist's detailing and perfection of facial features (eyes, eyebrows, nose, mouth) and his creation of continuous or broken planes, curves, and surfaces, the face becomes a wholly three-dimensional form. As the figure is turned in the hand and privately contemplated, the subtle dimensionalities of the face become fully evident and a continuous silhouette of its form is revealed. "The profiles are the silhouettes of the figure, according to the angle of our inspection from full front, from the rear, from above, below, right, or left. The variations of these silhouettes [are] illimitable, and they 'figure' space in a hundred different ways as we move about the sculpture" (Focillon 1992:77). The overall rendition of the proportions of the head, face, and body and then the delicate interpretation of shape and line, and of symmetry or asymmetry,[11] yield a form that in its aggregate volume and in its details is recognizable as a specific person. The Baule say approvingly of a well-sculpted figure, "It resembles a human being" (*o fa sran*), thereby choosing to emphasize its perception as a person rather than, specifically, as a man or woman.[12] Above all the sculptural interpretation of the face and the gaze creates verisimilitude, the realism of personhood.

Freedberg argues that "to perceive an image in terms of the intimate and familiar depends, in the first instance, on the perception of similitude. . . . [W]e empathize with an image because it shows a body like . . . ourselves; we feel close to it because of its similarity to our own physique and that of our neighbors" (1989:191). The Baule believe the *blolo* to be entirely equivalent to life "on this earth here" (*asie'n su wa*), and thus they perceive the otherworld man or woman of their dreams and reveries entirely in terms of similitude. The figure, besides making possible the imagining of this othermate, also makes possible, especially in the meditation of reverie, a critically important *self*-imagining.

> [S]elf-imaginings are crucial components of our imaginative experiences. It is chiefly by imagining ourselves facing certain situations, engaging in certain activities, observing certain events, experiencing or expressing feelings or attitudes that we come to terms with our feelings—that we discover them, learn to accept them, purge ourselves of them, or whatever exactly it is that imagining helps us to do. (Walton 1990:34)

As Westerners, we can only attempt to imagine the profound complexities of Baule imaginings of the otherworld. How does one begin to imagine the constancy of its distant presence, the timelessness of its existence, the profoundly private intimacy of one's relationship with the otherworld mate, and its embodiment of potentiality for things in the real world to be different? Dreams, we have argued, lead to daytime reveries, and both of these oneiric activities are constant and continual, week in and week out, as one seeks to live meaningfully in community. The *blolo* image, in its inherently human similitude, is the crucial prop in Baule imaginings of the otherworld.

Chapter Five

OUTSIDE IMAGININGS: THE OBJECT AS SOUVENIR

My task so far has been to examine an art genre *in situ* in its culture of origin and to reflect on the imaginings that brought specific works of art into being as well as the imaginings that in turn they themselves facilitated. Now I undertake an entirely different enterprise: the examination of the perception of this art in another milieu, and its created place in other systems of meaning. To look at the individually commissioned *blolo* image in relation to cultural and individual psychologies of meaning for the Baule, as we have done so far, is to deal with the artness of the object. To look at hundreds of these twentieth-century images as they become commodities (and inspire their own reproduction as replicas) in an international system of commerce is to look at the derived productive values of the material object. Yet the goal is still to investigate and understand the cultural creation of meaning, the need for the artwork, and the imaginings it facilitates. Does the modern Baule figure make possible the creation of alternate models of reality, even as commodity?

One of my pleasures over the years of my research on Baule figurative art has been the willingness of Baule people to talk about the *blolo,* its inhabitants, and their own firsthand experiences of this otherworld. The research undertaking has been very much the anthropology of everyday knowledge—the examination of ideas shared throughout Baule society—as opposed to an investigation of the private knowledge of any religious virtuosi or intellectual elite. The *blolo* has impinged on many Baule people at critical junctions in their lives, and the commissioning of *blolo* images has been widespread. Unlike the quite limited number of masks found in a given Baule village, one could find dozens and dozens of *blolo* figures in many villages. Many thousands of the figures have been carved over the past one hundred years, and many hundreds have ended up in museum and private collections of African art, where they are exhibited as exemplars of African aesthetics.

The willingness of the Baule people to part with figures through purchase

20. Figure of an other-world man as a war veteran (*ancien combattant*) wearing a forage cap bearing the insignia of the French troupes coloniales, a cross pendant, tank top, shorts, belt, and shoes, c. 1955, height 29 cm. Fowler Museum of Cultural History, University of California, Los Angeles, X94.62.18.

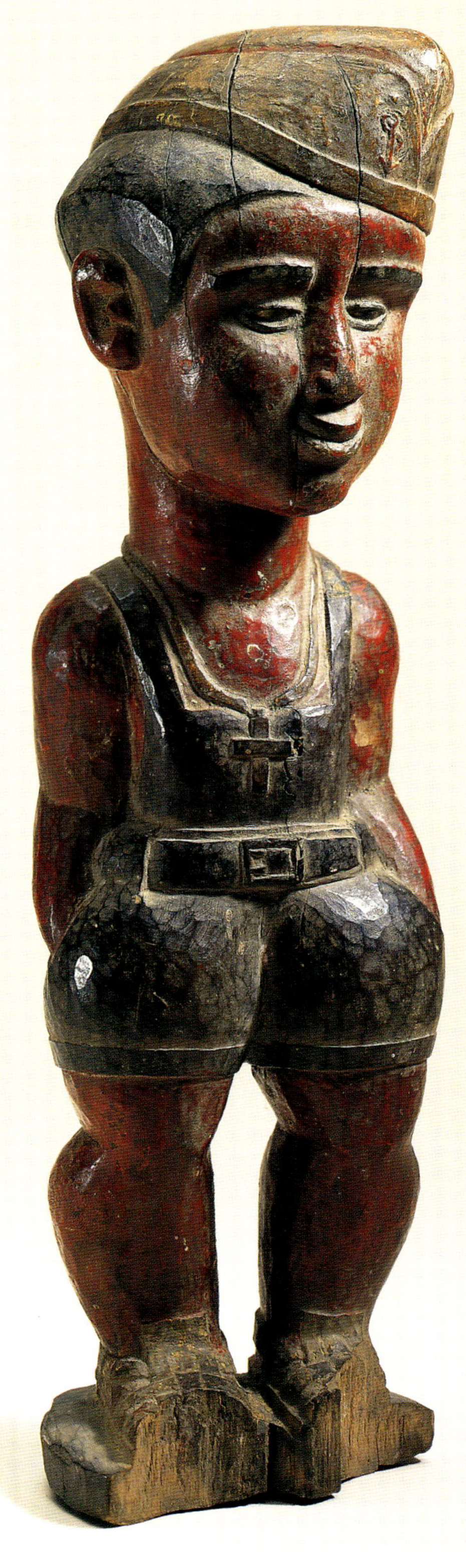

or barter has to be understood in terms of two ideas. First is the idea that the *blolo* figure is significant or useful only for the person who commissions it and cares for it; after his or her death it has no function except possibly as a memento of its deceased owner. Second, the figure is meaningful only in terms of its intermediary position in an *ongoing* relationship with the *blolo* partner; in the event that the crisis which precipitated its carving is not resolved, the efficacy of the figure may be called into question and thus it becomes superfluous. Thereafter, the figure may be neglected, becoming a mere carving, a plaything for children, an object that can be sold or traded to an outsider.

These ideas, internal to Baule society, are the necessary conditions that have made possible the exportation of *blolo* figures into Western collections. The essential condition, however, has been the active hunting for these figures by outsiders seeking economic gain. In the twentieth century, as Baule society has become ever more integrated into a world economic system, and the local economy has become increasingly monetarized, each natural and cultural product found in the Baule world can be seen in terms of its potential economic value. This economically reductionist state of affairs has existed for almost one hundred years. It is the direct result of colonization, colonialism, and the forced integration of Baule society into a world economy.

COLONIZATION AND ITS AFTERMATH IN BAULE SOCIETY

In the first decades of colonial subjugation, the period from 1889 to the eve of the World War II—from initial French penetration to the full "pacification" of the Baule in 1911 and the subsequent full imposition of colonial rule—Baule society and culture were subjected to ruthless and brutal domination.[1] In spite of waging one of the longest resistance struggles against colonization in Africa (see Crowder 1971:15), the Baule were finally brought to submission and became, in the words of Timothy Weiskel, "a tractable labor force in the service of the embryonic colonial economy" (1980:3). No longer were the Baule free agents creating and judging social meaning in terms of a local scale of values. They were suddenly and irrevocably thrust into a new world dominated by raw military, political, and economic power. For the Baule, as for other colonized Africans, "the years between 1900 and 1940 witnessed, on an unprecedented scale, transformations in social identity, cognitive systems and means of communication" (Roberts 1990:1). The Baule world became defined by external poles and agents of power: the colonially created *canton* and its *chef de canton,*[2] the district *poste* and its *chef*, the regional *cercle* and its *commandant*, the distant colonial capital and the *gouverneur*, and the far-off mother country and its government. At every level were the agents and institutions of economic change: tax collectors, buyers of wild rubber, petty traders, exporters, importers, colonial trading houses such as the Compagnie Française d'Afrique Occidentale, and the full apparatus of colonial government.

One indication of the brutal changes brought about under colonial domination—and a telling one for our own investigation of changes in Baule figurative art—is that of French conscription of African men for colonial and metropolitan armies. Myron Eschenberg, in *Colonial Conscripts: The "Tirailleurs Sénégalais" in French West Africa, 1857–1960,* states that "French military conscription in West Africa was indeed a tax in blood and sweat. Hundreds of thousands of young Africans were conscripted to serve overseas in European and colonial wars during the first half of this century. Still thousands more were drafted into . . . dreaded labor brigades" (1991:47). Forced recruitment for the army was paralleled by general recruitment of forced labor for the commercial development (*la mise en valeur*) of France's new colony of Côte d'Ivoire. The modern nation of Côte d'Ivoire, like few other West African countries apart from Ghana, is the result of a plantation economy based on coffee and cocoa (Chauveau and Dozon 1988:733). The Baule have been active participants in this new order since very early in this century.[3]

It is perhaps difficult for us to imagine the contrasts that must have distinguished traditional, and essentially local, subsistence economies from the unified and all inclusive monetarized economy of the developing colony with all of its attendant changes. It became an economy in which everyone was ultimately forced to participate because of obligatory head taxes that had to be paid in cash. Some of the changes included the new availability of European-produced consumer goods, especially industrially produced cloth, clothes, shoes, and headgear, and the new ubiquity of outside agents of colonial power. In the early colonial period a privileged class of Africans arose who, socially, occupied the middle ground between colonial masters and colonized subjects, moving back and forth between the foreign-dominated urban centers and the rural villages of Baule peasant farmers.[4]

Following colonization and the new realities abruptly and powerfully imposed on the Baule world early in this century, Baule figurative art depicting otherworld mates evolved significantly. As the real world was being irrevocably changed, so were ideas about the otherworld of the *blolo,* and it is not too surprising that its denizens came to be depicted in art with less scarification, with more clothing, and often in brighter hues achieved through the use of industrial paints rather than natural dyes (ill. 21). Female figures still often remained within a traditional canon, with their physical attributes and childbearing potential proudly displayed. But male statues were typically depicted in modern clothing and with other attributes gleaned from the modern Baule world and the wider world of Europe. Many male figures, for example,

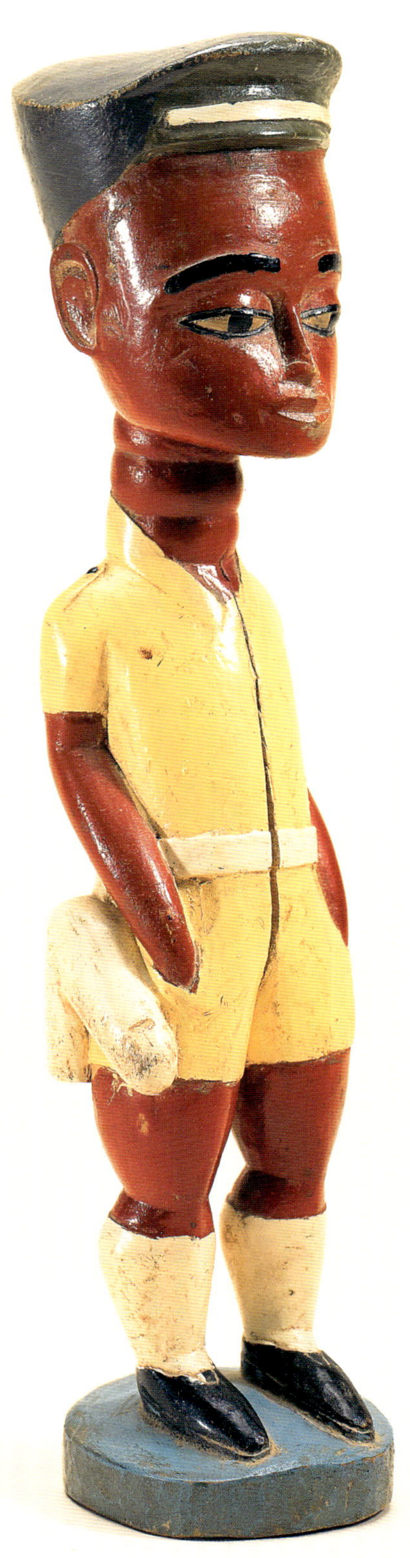

were depicted in different military uniforms or headgear, evoking an identity of the *ancien combattant,* whether in World Wars I and II or the French wars in Indochina (ill. 22).

THE MODERN BAULE OTHERWORLD FIGURE READ AS *COLON*

Whatever the cultural and psychological motivations that have led to the difference between the nudity of female figures and the clothed nature of male figures, the perception of these figures in the marketplace has also been one of difference. Females have been seen as depictions of traditional African women, whereas the males have been seen as postcolonization depictions of foreign men (see ills. 2, 4, 7, 20): the so-called *colon,*[5] or colonial (see Liking 1987).

It is important to examine the historical use and change in meaning of the French word *colon,* given the widespread confusion in the current literature devoted to this topic. Putative histories of the word abound, such as that put forth by Clémentine Deliss.

> Jens Jahn organized an exhibition of what he termed "Colon" art. Making a pun on the "colonization" of the African art market itself, Jahn grouped together African carvings from the late 19th and early 20th centuries [Jahn 1983]. The common theme was the European, ranging from the stereotypical soldier to the district officer and the missionary. (1991:14)

Jahn probably picked up the word *colon* from the evolving jargon of the West African art trade. In 1972, when I first became familiar with the art market in Côte d'Ivoire, the word *colon* was used by African art dealers to describe any work of art that through its form or painted surface showed a contemporary (in other words, nontraditional) character. The descriptive and, at that point, rather pejorative word *colon* was used in reference to clothed statues, any object depicting European accoutrements, or any type of art—masks, fly whisks, stools, combs—to which modern industrial paint had been applied.[6] The art marketeers in Côte d'Ivoire at that time were still largely hoping to find a traditional object of top quality. Works described by dealers at that time as *colon* were works of art that clearly were *not* in the market canon of *traditional* and therefore not as readily salable. *Colon* was in effect a residual category, a leftover from the gamut of "traditional" art forms.[7] Similarly, at the same time, the stylistic appellation *Lobi* was used to categorize minimally carved figures, no matter what their provenance, that were not easily categorized in terms of received notions of other named ethnic styles such as Baule, Guro, Yaure, or Senufo.[8]

At some point in the later 1970s there was a significant shift in the meaning of the word *colon.* It became restricted to a taxonomically independent

21. Figure of an otherworld man as a gendarme wearing a billed cap, uniform, and holstered pistol, c. 1965, height 30.3 cm. Fowler Museum of Cultural History, University of California, Los Angeles, X94.77.15.

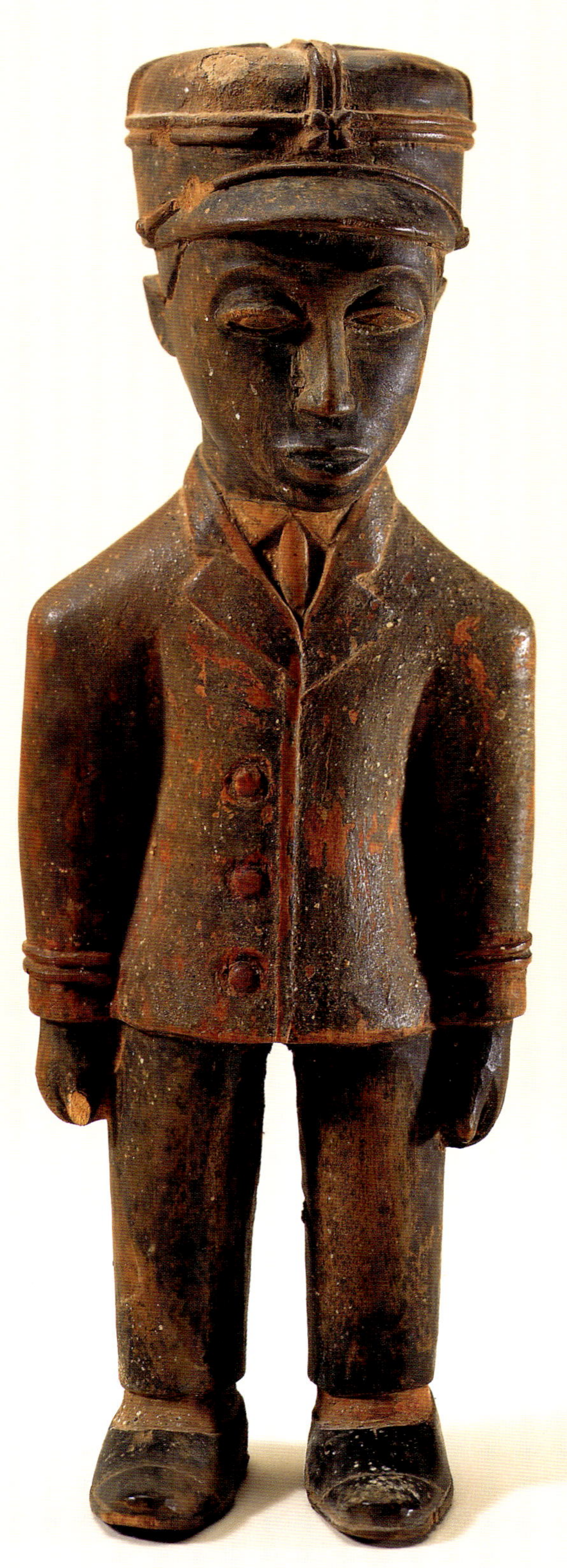

and newly valorized category of art that was now commercially viable: Baule figures depicted with modern clothes. Historical changes occurred in market attitudes toward a formerly underappreciated form of art. Finally, however, the *colon,* as both idea and object, achieved considerable popularity as its meaning was reinvented in the middle ground linking the African art dealer and the foreign buyer.

THE ART TRADE IN CÔTE D'IVOIRE, CA. 1960–1980

Who were the sellers and buyers of African art in Côte d'Ivoire in the sixties and the seventies, and what was the character of the market? The driving force of the market in those days was what still drives it: the goal of obtaining at low cost an authentic work of "traditional" art to be resold at some significant multiple of its purchase price. The market in that period was organized both geographically and hierarchically. Rural villages, the prime territory for prospection, were visited by itinerant buyers who more often than not attempted to extract works of art by bartering manufactured goods for them instead of buying them outright. Other buyers were the Dyula or Hausa[9] traders based in provincial towns who regularly visited a circuit of weekly village markets and who occasionally accepted art objects instead of money, subsequently exchanging the objects for money with other town-based art traders. The buyers of art *en brousse* (in the bush, as the rural sector has become known) were like buyers of any other commodity; their *modus operandi* was to buy and then resell as quickly as possible in order to extract a reasonable profit and continue buying. At this level of activity, traders had no inventory. The town traders, however, often held a certain stock that they dipped into for resale to yet other dealers who visited them from the cities of Bouaké, Korhogo, Man, or Abidjan. The art dealers in these provincial cities had both retail and wholesale clients: local expatriate collectors or other dealers. At the end of the line in Abidjan were the major expatriate collectors and dealers in prime objects who in turn selected the *crème de la crème* from this production for their own collections or as inventory for resale to European and American dealers.

22. Figure of an other-world man as "soldier" (sonja) with military cap, c. 1950, height 24.5 cm. Fowler Museum of Cultural History, UCLA, X94.62.20.

Most of the major expatriate collectors in Abidjan were, in effect, also dealers. In their quest for art that interested them, they often bought other objects of lesser interest or quality in order to maintain relationships with dealers who might in the future deliver more important objects. These collectors were continually culling their collections by offering certain objects to other established or novice collectors, friends, or visitors. These collector-dealers often displayed the available objects in the quasi-public space of the living room, and kept the real collection in a private room elsewhere in the house or apartment, such as the master bedroom. They took the most significant acquisitions of the year home at the time of annual leave. Certain expatriate dealers in Abidjan ultimately contributed to the breakdown of the former structured situation by significantly raising prices and encouraging finders to bypass the various middlemen traders.

The top end of the art market in Côte d'Ivoire has always been a very small percentage of the total market in terms of volume of objects; the superb Dan mask is as hard to find as the exceptional American modernist painting, even if workmanlike examples of both can be found in quantity. The hunting-and-gathering approach to traditional arts and crafts has, however, delivered to the marketplace a tremendous quantity of objects hitherto overlooked. One example of such a discovery in Côte d'Ivoire and its neighboring countries has been furniture: beds, washing tables, stools, and chairs. Another has been the modern Baule figure offered in the guise of the *colon*.

To concentrate principally on the sellers of art in Côte d'Ivoire would be to neglect the impact of the buyers and the historic dialogue between the two. Recent research on the Ivorian art market by Christopher Steiner (1991, 1994) provides a glimpse into the Abidjan art market of the late 1980s, but despite its considerable merits it is flawed by an approach that is almost completely ahistorical and quite artificially limited in its scope. Steiner neglects the postindependence realities of Côte d'Ivoire from the mid-1960s to the mid-1980s, the years of the so-called Ivorian miracle, and in effect limits the art market actors to the stereotypical social characters of local trader and foreign tourist. In the period of Côte d'Ivoire's economic boom, however, there was a massive, resident expatriate presence of businessmen, diplomats, and development experts, notably the corps of French *coopérants,* or technical assistants, that dominated some sectors of Ivorian government ministries such as secondary school education. In the 1970s the expatriate French population numbered some fifty thousand (den Tuinder 1978:124), peaking at near sixty thousand at the end of that decade prior to a downturn in the local economy and a concurrent reorientation of French government policy on overseas technical assistance. This continuous presence ten to eleven months per year is to be contrasted with the short-term visits of tourists; in 1968 tourists numbered only twenty-two thousand and their numbers did not exceed fifty thousand per year until 1971 (p. 52).

The resident expatriate population was also at this period the best-paid group in the entire nation. In the private sector economy, whose expatriate supervisors and managers outnumbered Ivorians by three to two, the top 20 percent of the labor force received 53.5 percent of total salary payments. This same pattern held in the public and parapublic sectors, where the top 20 percent received 56 percent of total salary payments (den Tuinder 1978:52). Taking into account other perquisites of expatriate contractual status, such as

23. Figure of an otherworld man as a colonial-era administrator wearing a pith helmet, colonial uniform, and boots. The coat collar mimics the neck lines often depicted on figures. C. 1930. Height 28.8 cm. Fowler Museum of Cultural History, University of California, Los Angeles, X94.62.24.

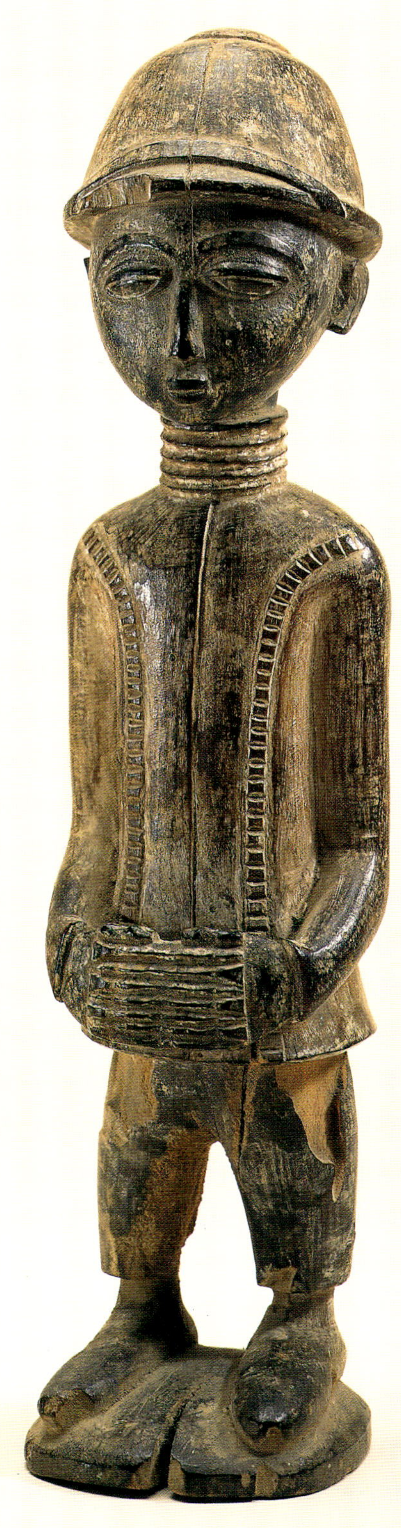

free housing, school allowances, and annual paid home leave, one glimpses the privileged life of the expatriate. I would argue that the resident expatriate was the principal actor in the Ivorian art market; his role as buyer has to be taken into account for any historical understanding of the market in the 1960s, 1970s, and early 1980s.

Throughout the 1970s and well into the 1980s I was both participant and observer in the expatriate community that was courted assiduously by art dealers as they created and cultivated individual networks of clients. Like art dealers anywhere, they catered to the particular interests, likes, and dislikes of their clients, knowing where their best chances lay for selling particular types of objects. Each client was also asked for referrals to other potential clients, always of course with the understanding that one would be presented new merchandise before the friends who had been recommended. These postindependence development experts and technical assistants—whom we could call the "new Africa hands" as opposed to the "old Africa hands" of an earlier period—were the ones who came to embrace what they perceived to be colonial statues, and it was their acquisitive interest, I am convinced, that in effect created and maintained the new valorization of the market category of *colon*.

No longer a characterization of all types of contemporary works of traditional types of art, the word *colon* began to be used as an explanatory "sales pitch" for a new category of art that was on the same footing as other known categories, such as the so-called ancestor figure. The clothed Baule figure became a commercially viable commodity and an object of choice for the expatriate's local apartment as well as a prized souvenir to be taken back to Europe on annual leave (ill. 23). It was, with the proper explanation, both old and new; it was a sample of the old and authentic Africa of the colonial period, and at the same time it was a fashionably new type of souvenir, supposedly known and appreciated only by "insiders," and undiscovered or unappreciated by common tourists. In the 1960s and 1970s, tourists sought out traditional art, even if these were only commercially reproduced replicas of traditional forms.[10] In the 1990s, of course, the *colon*, now presented and perceived as a historical artifact, has also become a commercial viable category of traditional art that is offered for sale to tourists (Steiner 1994:148–54).

THE *COLON* AND THE INVENTION OF HISTORY

24. A shop selling so-called *colon* figures. Dakar, Senegal, 1993. Photograph by the author.

The *colon* was an invention, a projection, and a voluntary misperception of history by those resident foreign experts, *coopérants,* and diplomats who were newly discovering Africa. They seized upon these clothed statuettes as evidence of an imagined preindependence history, as illustration of an essentially benign colonialism, almost an inevitable event in world history, whose agents

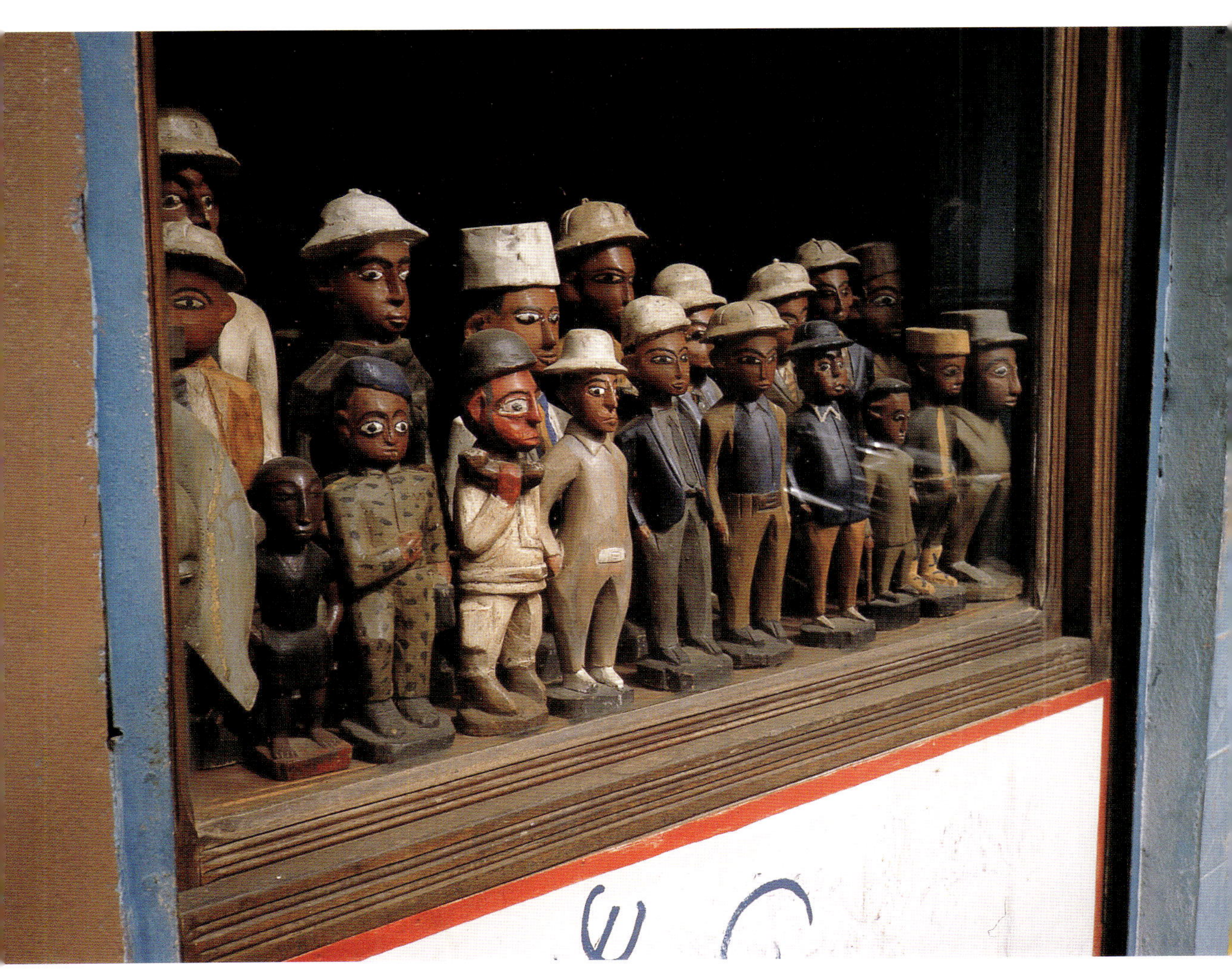

were lone individuals. As the formerly unsalable modern Baule figures became popular, demand finally outstripped supply, and the effect was the production of replica forms: new statuettes in the putative colonial style.

The genesis of this new *colon* genre arose, I am convinced, from a misreading of the clothed Baule figure, from a failure to comprehend the attributes so readily understandable from the Baule point of view.[11] The military uniform and headgear that to the Baule connoted the identity of *sonja*, the *ancien combattant* of the French colonial army (see ills. 20, 22), were seen by the "outside eye" as a proof that the figure depicted a colonial personage. The use of red paint to color the skin of the unclothed areas of the modern figure—in order to indicate a skin tone of light or red, according to Baule concepts—was interpreted as an intent to depict the skin of a white man. In their totality, the features of the clothed Baule figure were assumed to indicate that it had been created in the colonial (that is, pre-1960) era as a depiction of a foreign man: the colonial agent, the *colon*. In the context of this "appreciation," the outsider simply did not understand visual clues in the same way that the insider did. Instead of seeing the clothed figure as a contemporary and ongoing phenomenon, they saw it as a historical product, an authentic object from the past, and thus salable.

The dialogue between African seller and foreign buyer, ably described by Steiner (1994), has been mutually reinforcing. The foreign buyer has wanted to believe that he is acquiring a work of "real" African art, the seller has catered to this desire, and traders have often artificially aged these statuettes in order to pass them off as antique (p. 151). The tourist buyer of a *colon* wants to acquire real local art in the same way that he has undertaken the touristic quest for the real and the authentic experience that, as MacCannell (1989) argues, motivated his foreign travel in the first place. The feedback effect of the discourse between African seller and foreign buyer has ultimately led to the development and florescence of the *colon* genre with its ever more detailed depictions of colonial attributes. A certain postcolonial kitschiness has developed in the genre. "Kitsch objects . . . are apprehended on the level of collective identity. They are souvenirs of an era and not of a self" (Stewart 1984:167). The serial and kitschlike character of the genre, and the marketplace alignment of multiple, workshop-produced copies of the pith-helmeted, suited, accoutrement-bedecked male figure (see ill. 24), apparently have interfered little with the purchase of these objects as souvenirs of the imagined colonial past. Stewart quotes Jean Baudrillard to the effect that "kitsch represents a saturation of the object with details," but she argues that "it would be more accurate to say that the kitsch object offers a saturation of materiality, a saturation that takes place to such a degree that materiality is ironic, split into contrasting voices: past and present, mass production and individual subject, oblivion and reification."

History has been turned back on itself to invent the *colon*. Authentic Baule figures in modern dress have been carved by Baule artists working creatively within their own culturally determined aesthetic canon and evidently relishing the chance to depict the art of fashion (see, e.g., ills. 2, 4, 9). Although clothes may be carved or painted on these figures, their facial and corporal aesthetics are clearly in accord with precolonial styles, even if the Western concept of the waist is at times depicted. The new *colon* genre, however, is far more fanciful, even to the point of overkill. Fully dressed-up in suit, vest, tie, pith helmet, and shoes, figures often hold in their hands a European accoutrement such as a cane, a whip, a gun, or a gin bottle. The result has been that in the past twenty years a totally new genre has been invented. From an initial revivalism that reproduced the perceived hallmarks of the *colon* genre (pith helmet, military uniform, shirts, shorts, sandals, and bright paint), artistic creativity has led to stylistic involution, a self-conscious attempt to innovate, extend, and improve the genre. In the words of *colon* sculptors interviewed by Wéréwéré Liking:

> For me, *colon* statuary is first of all a sculpture which allows us to go further in our work. We can introduce modern products, and apply ourselves to transforming them in order to create our own nuances, our patinas, and conceive other, more modern sculptures, even if they are not exactly *colon* figures. (Dian Lafia, quoted by Liking 1987:19)

> I have found a lot of tricks. I invent models, add gadgets, discover new styles that I am commissioned to make and that enrich my inspiration. (Anonymous artist, p. 17)

The word *colon* has by now been used indiscriminately in both the marketplace and the literature as a category that includes both authentic works of art and replicas. From the initially descriptive mode in which the word was used by African dealers in the late sixties and early seventies, it has evolved as a concept to explain and, above all, to sell figurative art, whether old or new, that incorporates elements of Western fashion. When the hunting-and-gathering approach to supplying *colon* goods failed to meet market hunger, it was replaced by the domestication of production. A specifically engineered standard product is now delivered to the marketplace, where it is eagerly purchased by consumers conditioned to accept a new exotic taste.[12]

THE *COLON* AND THE NEED FOR NARRATIVE

From the progressive escalation of dialogue between buyers and sellers there has emerged a mutually reinvented history. This is a history that conveniently concentrates on, and gives great emphasis to, details—as in the concern for the detailed "portrait" of an individual colonial—while effectively obfuscating the harsher and more painful aspects of the larger picture of colonialism: lack of individual liberty, coerced recruitment into an economic and social world defined by others, and the overthrow of a heretofore sufficient cosmology. This invented nostalgic history also conveniently obscures postcolonial realities, including the reality, political independence notwithstanding, of still being peripheral to the Euro-American dominated world—still being, in effect, a commercial colony, a source of natural products and a pool of labor. The overwhelming majority of made-for-the-marketplace *colons* are male. The narrative, whether implicit or explicit, that has been generated around their invented history has projected that which is foreign or colonial as male and cultural, and that which is African as female and natural. The basic assumption has been that the clothed male must be (a depiction of) a European and the unclothed female an African. An interesting illustration of this naïve assumption is found in Julius Lips's discussion, in *The Savage Hits Back* (1937), of a Kongo carving of a man and woman. It matters little that both figures have fully comparable physiognomies and stances and that the described manner of interlinking the arms is found on traditional objects from the mid-nineteenth century.[13]

> [H]ere a white man is portrayed with his black woman, and we note that she has already learned to pass her arm in European fashion under his. Except for a small skirt, a strap passing round the neck and breast, and an armlet, she is clad in nothing but a native tattoo-pattern, whilst the white man is wearing a wing-shaped elongated jacket. . . . The European is wearing a round hat, has bare feet like his companion, and is fixed on a white, while she is on a black, socle, the two supports resting on a common base. (1937:131–32)

Among Baule figures identified as being produced by a single artist, one may find male figures that are clothed and female figures that are unclothed, and although contemporaneous, the male figures may be interpreted in the art market as modern or *colon,* whereas the female figures may be construed as traditional. The *colon* market has even led to the creation of *colon* genre groupings of a white man and an African woman. But whether as genre figures or as individual figures, the contrasting pair of modern male-as-*colon* and female-as-African has been associated with a narrative content that tells the story of the colonial period in terms of a fundamental, multilayered series of oppositions, namely: male is to female as foreigner is to African, as colonizer is to colonized, as historical is to traditional, as urban is to rural, as clothed is to unclothed, as dominating is to dominated, as active is to passive. A quite peculiar view of West African and Ivorian history has been thus read from the *colon* genre; it is as though an outside male gaze had constructed Africa itself as the female body: naturally fecund, potentially productive, fully available, and only in need of a master.

This invented, revisionist history of colonialism has dramatically downplayed its political violence and domination while stressing a presumed levity of African humor concerning the white man assumed to be depicted in the *colon* figure. In this regard the words of a former schoolteacher turned *colon* carver are most interesting. He says of the commerce in brand-new *colon* figures that

> it makes one forget the bad side of colonialism. Every time I go by the [art] market on the Plateau, and I see people buying my *colons,* I remark that they are happy. They ask amusing questions; *they want to forget the past.* It's like a medicine against bad memories. It's really a sculpture of friendship. It changes everyone's mind-set. (Liking 1987:17; my translation with emphasis added)

The assumption that the *colon* demonstrates an African sense of humor harks back to the notion first advanced by Julius Lips in the mid-1930s that African figures depicted in Western clothes represented the white man and were intended as critical commentary. "The peculiar illustrations of foreigners from Europe and America show us also that the colored man has seen through the white man's world, that he understands its weaknesses and faults" (p. 58). The reading of the *colon* in terms of an intended irony, caricature, or more generally as humor has become widespread and taken as truth.

> These little characters called "Colons" are the witness of a movement from the bush to Western civilization. Unlike primitive art, *colon* art forsakes conceptual ideas of human representation and stigmatizes the individual in seizing the pose, the expression or the particularity of clothing.
>
> These colons have a sense of humor and are often real miniature *chefs d'oeuvre* which have a special place between naïve art, popular art, and that of caricature. (Binoche et Godeau 1987:3; my translation)

In these figures made in response to foreign demand and intentionally created as *colons,* carvers, too, now seek to reinvent the past. Another commercial carver, Dian Lafia, states that

> when one is African, colonization is a thing of such importance that one cannot *not* look at it. With everything recounted to us by our old men, we try to reflect and create something at our own level. And when my father, who lived through colonization, sees what we are making, he remembers other details which in turn enrich our inspiration. For me, I am impassioned by history, the actions of the colonials,

> the authority they had over the Blacks. . . . Thus I get inspiration from old styles in order to maintain history. One has to remember. (Liking 1987:18; my translation)

The history that is maintained, however, is an obfuscation of colonial history. Its distortions are paralleled in the mystification of the history of the *colon* genre itself, and like the *colon* its details are fanciful inventions. Liking, in her self-consciously promotional book, *Statues colons,* goes so far as to argue that in the rural sector

> the majority of the old men who were depositories of ancestral knowledge are dead. Those who remain have so few occasions to use their memory that they end up by losing it.
>
> . . . For the functions of the *colon* in the societies of yesterday, we were [thus] obliged to address ourselves to old art dealers, collectors and sellers of objects. (1987:13)

Choosing to believe that the originators of the form have lost their history, she recounts and takes at face value a myth of origin invented by some dealers, namely, that the *colon* is an example of the so-called *photo africaine* genre—figures that were allegedly commissioned by African clients as depictions of the colonial white man. This new tale of origin seeks to situate the *colon* genre as authentically African and serves to deny any idea that these works of art might arise from foreign demand. It resituates original intentionality into an imagined context of the African regarding the European as Other. In effect, the story introduces a sophisticated notion of irony; the object is seen as embodying incongruity—the incongruity of the colonially dominated being able to anticipate the ultimate impotence of colonialism. Prior to the onslaught of history and the inevitability of African political independence, the male agent of imperialism and colonialism, as seen in the *colon,* is a pitiful figure, lost in his soon-to-be-outmoded trappings of power. As overemphasized accoutrement on the *colon,* the pith helmet—which as actual object worn by foreigners in the colonial period had implicitly evoked colonial power and also the conquest of nature by culture, science, and reason—becomes a poor theatrical prop of laughably outmoded fashion, a thing of nostalgia.

In discussing the idea and the status of those objects subsumed under the category *colon,* it becomes necessary to deal with notions of intentionality and autonomy in the created object. When the Baule otherworld figure, whether clothed or unclothed, is the result of a commission between a Baule client and a Baule artist, it can be categorized as authentic.[14] It exists because it was created as an individual, objectified response to an existential need. In terms of the intentionality that subtends it, it was made as a representative of a person in the otherworld, and as object it creates a new reality—a new *knowledge*—that exists independent of any words. It does something that words alone cannot do, and it becomes autonomous. "[A]rtworks are in themselves without movement and life and yet—with or without regard to how they are 'used'—they often appear to be inhabited by a sort of 'autonomous' life, by something that depends as much on the way they were conceived as their formal 'strength'" (Pellizzi 1990–91:5). Although it can be described and talked about through words, the figure is a work of art, and it is not, in the final argument, dependent on any mythology of words. There is, in fact, "a *silence* at the core of that kind of doing which we name 'art.'" The autonomy of the object arises, however, within a particular cultural locus. Baxandall, in arguing for the quattrocento painting as the "deposit of a social relationship," points out that both artist and patron "worked within institutions and conventions—commercial, religious, perceptual, in the widest sense social—that were different from ours and influenced the forms of what they together made" (1972:1). So, too, the Baule artist and client "join in a common imagining" that leads to the creation of a figure that both see, read, and understand with the same *cultural eye*. The silence of the figure makes possible private imaginings because, as autonomous object, it articulates and complements the implicit ideas, incipient experiences, and otherwise inchoate emotions of its owner vis-à-vis the otherworld.

The clothed modern Baule *blolo* figure is also the model that through outsider perception has been reinvented as the *colon*. It has served as a source of inspiration in the invention of a new type of art, the *colon*-as-souvenir.

> [T]his capacity of objects to serve as traces of authentic experience is . . . exemplified by the souvenir. The souvenir distinguishes experiences. . . . [W]e need and desire souvenirs of events that are reportable, events whose materiality has escaped us, events that exist only through the invention of narrative. *Through narrative the souvenir substitutes a context of perpetual consumption for its context of origin.* It represents not the lived experience of its maker but the "secondhand" experience of its possessor/owner. . . . The souvenir speaks to a context of origin through a *language of longing,* for it is not an object arising out of need or use value; it is an object arising out of the necessarily insatiable demands of nostalgia. The souvenir generates a narrative that only reaches "behind," spiraling in a continually inward movement rather than outward toward the future. (Stewart 1984:134; emphasis added)

Stewart's approach to the souvenir, and more generally to "objects of desire," is extremely relevant to our attempt to understand the reinvention of the Baule *blolo* image as the *colon*. The former is an object specifically created for a real individual need; it is an essential, material response to a problem of the lived *now.* The latter is an object speculatively created to satisfy general nostalgia for an imaginary past; it is an ephemeral curiosity that seeks to move history into private time (p. 138) and thereby depict an imaged *then.* As with other antinomical dualities, however, the contrast between authentic and replica Baule figures does not always hold, for the differences are less those of essence than of the imaginings occasioned by the object and the narratives generated around the object.

The problem of asserting and maintaining an absolute distinction in the interpretation of the two forms of figurative art that we are discussing, *blolo* figure and *colon,* is that ultimately one is forced to admit that each, in its own way, serves to articulate, in Stewart's words, "a language of longing." Each serves to create or "authenticate a past or otherwise remote experience and, at the same time, to discredit the present" (1984:134). Each functions as a prop for imagining. The difference therefore lies not so much in the objects *qua* objects—even if I would still argue that there are very real differences between them—but in the differences of their original intentionalities and the narrative(s) invented around each object. Indeed, authentic *blolo* images may often have been categorized as *colon* and as such appropriated as souvenirs. The original imagining, lost when alienated from its original owner, gives way to a new narrative invented for the object by its new possessor. Art thus becomes souvenir.

Thus I return to the idea of the autonomy of the object. And it is here, perhaps, that I feel the need to articulate what at this moment is perhaps only a matter of personal belief: the idea that, whether in Africa or the West, the necessity of art and the power of art are due to the ultimate inadequacy of words. And now one can come back to an earlier *a priori*—that there *is* a difference between the real Baule *blolo* image and the replicative *colon.* The former, I believe, exists independent of words and creates meaning in its encoded autonomy; the latter is overly, and almost entirely, dependent on words. It does not create meaning; rather, meaning is imputed to it through a verbally ostensive decoding. It is not autonomous; it is dependent on the narrative brought to it. It is used as a created souvenir of events "whose materiality has escaped us, *events that exist only through the invention of narrative*" (Stewart 1984:134; emphasis added). Given that for the *colon* these events are themselves invented, then the object—as a reinvention of nonevents—turns out to be a secondary phenomenon, a symptom of a diseased view of history. It is an imagined thing serving as illustration to an imaginary something else. The souvenir replica "will not function without the supplementary narrative discourse that both attaches it to its origins and creates a myth with regard to those origins. What is this narrative of origins? It is a narrative of interiority and authenticity. It is not a narrative of the object; *it is a narrative of its pos-*

sessor" (p. 136). The *colon* serves as a prop to a skewed vision of the real world—a world of the past that is articulated and interpreted by its possessor. It is not an alternative to that world; rather it serves as a replica token. Its truthfulness turns out to be fictive. Although it may create narrative, it cannot, in the final analysis, create cosmic reverie.

Chapter Six

VEHICLES OF REVERIE

The title of this chapter is drawn from a passage in Charles Simic's poetically recounted reflections on the artistry of Joseph Cornell, *Dime-Store Alchemy: The Art of Joseph Cornell* (1992). In his discussion of the ways in which works of art may be invested with meaning or even life, Simic summons up the idea of the work of art as "a vehicle of reverie, an object that could enrich the imagination of the viewer and keep him company forever" (p. 44). This evocative notion serves as a poetic summing up of what I have sought to do in this book: examine the work of art in terms of its viewer and the imaginings it provokes. The meaning of the object has been sought in its original context of contemplation and appreciation.

To consider the work of art as a vehicle of reverie is to allow for a point of view that admits fully both what the object is and what it does, that is, to accept the object as both resultant product of the artist's ingenuity and as generative cause in the viewer's experience. There is a dynamic flow of creativity that leads from an initial imagining to the creation of the object, and later from the created object itself to new imaginings. The artist's private vision is channeled into the revelation of the form of the object; his insight, ideas, emotions, and unarticulated thoughts result in a new thing never before perceived and never before experienced. The artist's touch "represents a single moment in which the tool awakens form in its substance" (Focillon 1992:109). The awakened form of the created object, in turn, stimulates the imagination of the viewer-possessor in the construction of a new world seen privately in the mind's eye—a world that is in constant invention. In the object

> lies the creative originality that extracts from the substances furnished by nature all the matters necessary for *a new nature*. This originality is, moreover, one that unceasingly renews itself. For the matter, or substance, of an art is not a fixed datum that has been acquired once and for all. From its very first appearance it is transformation and novelty, because artistic activity, like a chemical reaction, elabo-

25. Figure of an other-world woman with a modern "extensions" hairstyle and neck lines, and wearing earrings, dress, necklace, watch, handbag, and high-heel shoes, c. 1965, height 39.5 cm. Fowler Museum of Cultural History, University of California, Los Angeles, X94.17.5.

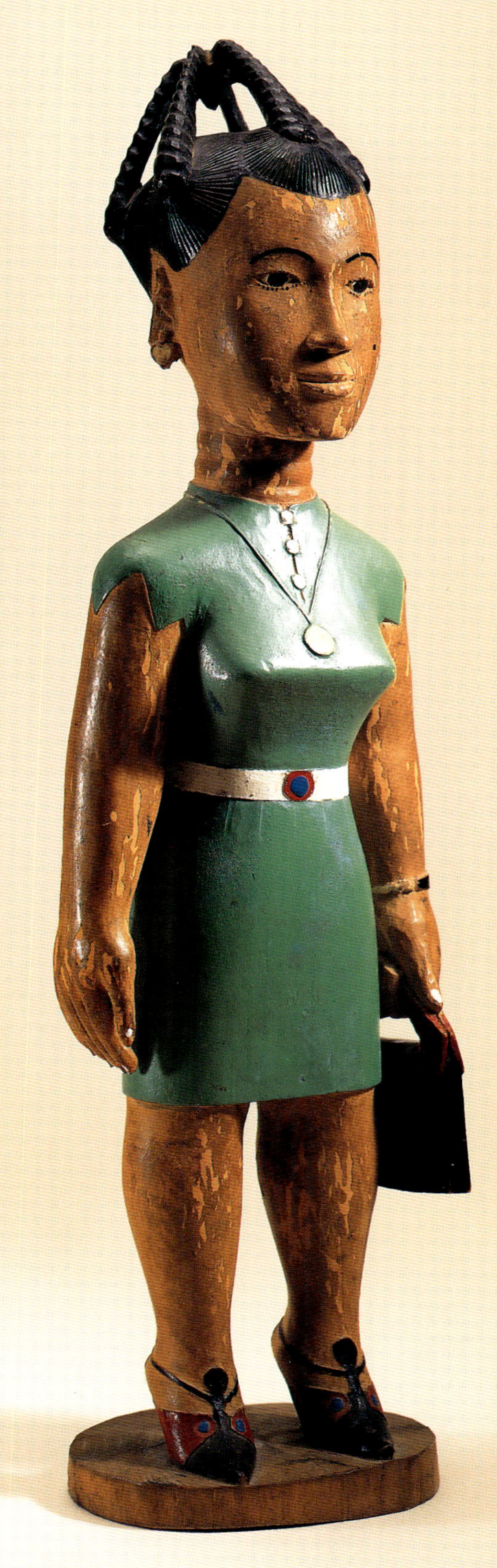

rates matter even as it continues the work of metamorphosis. (P. 99; emphasis added)

For the Baule, the figure of the otherworld mate is indeed a new nature—a person in wood who is, through reverie, an agent of metamorphosis. The sculpted figure links one inexorably to an infatuated partner who may well "keep [one] company forever"—the inamorata or inamorato of reverie who is also the lover in one's dreams. In that world, the *other*world, one finds a new identity; one becomes someone else in being quite differently defined by the secret mate. The private, individualized reality of the otherworld is experienced in dreams, is made real in their recounting, is apprehended anew in reverie, but is *perceived* through the senses in the physical object, the *blolo* image. The image makes real, maintains, and unceasingly renews the imagined world. There is a fundamental importance of the actual carving that represents the *blolo* mate in the imagining of the otherworld and in the living-out of the alliance found therein. The *blolo* image transforms mere wood into something new.

> [T]here is between the matters or substances of art and the substances of nature a divorce. . . . A new order is established, within which there are two distinct realms. . . . The wood of the statue is no longer that of the tree. . . . The color, the integument, all the values that affect the sight have changed. Things without a surface, whether once hidden behind the bark, buried in the mountain, imprisoned in the nugget or swallowed in the mud, have become wholly separated from chaos. *They have acquired an integument; they adhere to space; they welcome the daylight that works freely on them.* . . . [T]he life that seems to inhabit matter has undergone metamorphosis. (Focillon 1992:97; emphasis added)

The word *integument,* with its sense of "natural covering, as a skin," is particularly apt in thinking about the *blolo* image, for the surface of the image affects sight by evoking a being within. The figure as integumentary volume has a constitutive reality, not only culturally but also individually.

The specific *blolo* image exists at two different levels of reality: as cultural object and as individual event. The image makes concrete, or reifies, the general cultural abstraction known as *blolo,* and at the same time it serves to articulate a particular experience. The existence of the figure as image is contingent on the generalized Baule belief in an otherworld inhabited by human spirits, some of whom are indissolubly linked to real people as their mystic mates. The actual, created form of the figure brings the otherworld into life here on earth by making incarnate a specific otherworld person in a figure that manifests his or her personhood and attributes—physical, social, and individual. The *blolo* image represents the otherworld in miniature and in singularity. To the cultural eye the figure conveys verisimilitude—the recogni-

26. Figure of an otherworld man wearing a shirt, sharply creased trousers, and shoes. The hair is in a modern barbershop style, and the long neck has emphatic beauty lines. C. 1960. Height 35.5 cm. National Museum of African Art, anonymous gift, 93-1-3.

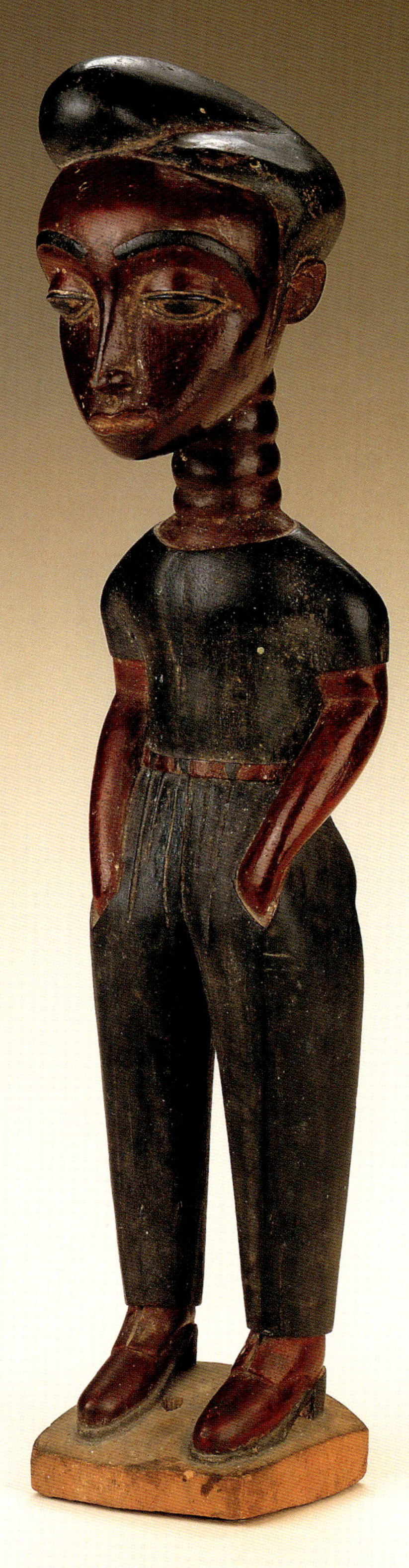

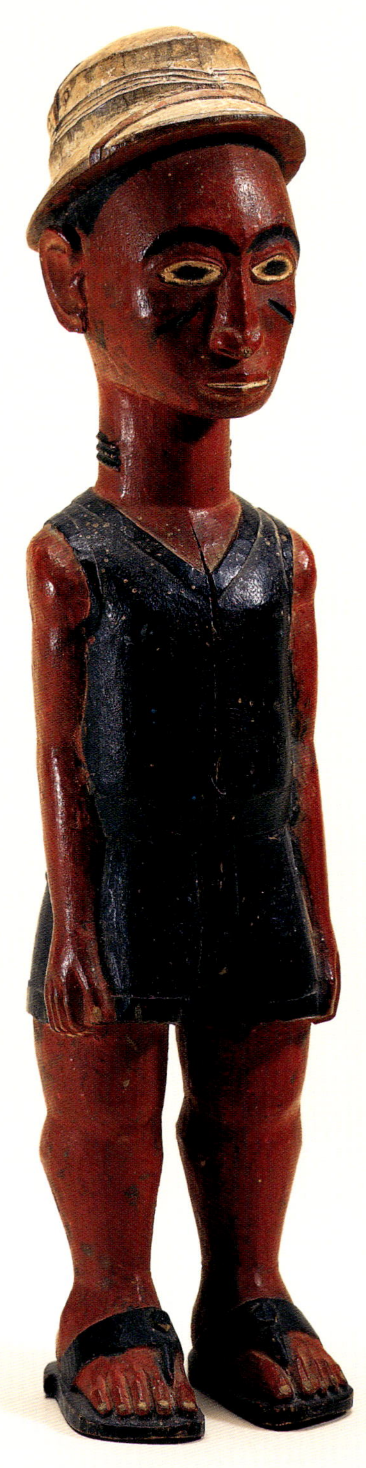

tion of a living presence—through its miniaturized portrayal of bodily volume and culturally determined human beauty. Furthermore, through its specificity and emphatic attention to details, especially those of the head and face, the figure makes manifest the individual personhood of the otherworld mate (ill. 26).

The artist's hands create a miniature embodiment of human physical perfection; the owner's eyes invest the figure with the full dimensionality of human personality. In the act of consecration the figure becomes an *image* with a recognized meaning. It is no longer just a sculpture, it is a sculptural likeness of an otherwise invisible being and as such is able to assume the role of an intermediary stand-in. Through the image, the relationship is established and sustained. In the articulations of its form and the unity of its surface, the image takes on a life and imposes itself on its viewer as a concrete entity to be encountered.

The autonomous existence of works of art is puzzling. The image is both highly specific to its context of origin, and yet able to escape it and live independently. It is a created *thing*, yet in its newness it is alive and it confronts us. The seeming contradictions of the status of the work of art have led Focillon to muse that

> [a] work is immersed in the whirlpool of time; and it belongs to eternity. A work of art is specific, local, and individual; and it is our brightest token of universality. A work of art rises proudly above any interpretation we may see fit to give it; and, although it serves to illustrate history, man and the world itself, it goes further than this; it creates man, creates the world and sets up history in an immutable order. (1992:32)

The created thing creates. The thing imagined becomes the thing that is seen *and* the thing that fixes us with its gaze. The work of art is made to be looked at, for art is a visual experience that differs profoundly from the experience of spoken words. Words, mere words, are inadequate to deal with art's independent reality. One is reduced to approximations, attempts at imaginings. One strives for a new poetics. One seeks to deal with the object in its own terms, not as illustration of some other reality or historical moment but as an independent, confrontational "new nature." Perhaps poetry itself is the appropriate metaphor. Poetry, after all, is at one level merely words, and therefore one may assume that in understanding its component parts one understands the whole, and can decode its content. In fact, the power of poetry is to be found in the uniqueness of its total form; words, cadences, alliterations, resonances, images, allusions, rhythms, and rhymes all build into the spoken power of poetry. Its power results from the originality and integrity of its form and thus its difference from other forms of communication.

27. Figure of an otherworld man with facial and neck scarification, and wearing a colonial-era pith helmet, shirt, shorts, and sandals, c. 1950, height 28 cm. Fowler Museum of Cultural History, University of California, Los Angeles, X94.62.9.

The work of art also derives its power from its uniqueness; although it may have elements that are similar to other works within the same style, its power lies in its individuality. Unfortunately, in much African art history the work of art has all too often been regarded reductively: as typical of a cultural style and genre, as illustrating social phenomena or culturally constructed cosmology, as reflecting social realities, or as illuminating other aspects of culture. The autonomy and the specificity of the work of art have often been denied. It has been reduced to epiphenomenon, derived from other realities and incapable of effect. The *experienced* work of art is, of course, something entirely different. In Focillon's apt phrasing, it is "a new nature," an "attempt to express something . . . unique," an "affirmation of something . . . whole, complete, absolute. . . . [It is] both matter and mind, both form and content" (1992:31). It is brought into being because it is needed; nothing can substitute for it.

The recourse to art as a solution to sexual, marital, or social crises of the type experienced by a Baule woman or man fascinates and intrigues me. Through the specifically commissioned work of art, an imagined world is imaged, and the image, the living presence, creates other imaginings. The surface of the *blolo* image becomes the virtual surface of the otherworld itself. The sculptured *blolo* figure is all about surface, the integrity and boundedness of the integument. "The character of sculpture," Focillon states, "must, in one way or another, be that of a solid, irrespective of its protrusions and irrespective of whether it is composed on a single plane or as a statue around which one can move" (1992:76–77). The volumes of sculpture "depend on light—on the light that models them, that brings out the solids or the voids and that makes the surface the expression of a relative density" (p. 102). The surface of the solid sculpture that is the Baule figure is perceived and appreciated by both sight and touch; the figure is held and moved by its owner-spectator so that eye and hand experience it simultaneously. Through the image in its immediacy, he or she can perceptibly encounter the person of the otherworld and vicariously imagine his or her existence, presence, and fullness of being. Albeit a wooden person, the figure *is* a person who makes communication possible.

It is by now clear that in my use of the word *image* I have sought to examine the Baule *blolo* figure in terms of how it is intended to create a sense of individual personhood and how it is perceived as conveying this verisimilitude (ill. 27). I have been greatly influenced by Freedberg and his approach to "the relations between images and people in history" (1989:xix). My task has been to imagine what might be the response—the private imaginings—of a Baule man or woman as he or she gazes at the figure that evokes the presence of an otherwise invisible partner of the opposite sex. What are the ideas, thoughts, and emotions that are brought to life as the figure is privately and silently contemplated? When the artist focuses his skills in the awakening of form from raw wood, his lived experience and culturally mediated worldview are brought to bear in each touch of his adze and knife. His notions of beauty, his understanding of maleness and femaleness, his ideas about village life and society, his memories of youthfulness, and his own sexual history all merge as he imagines into being the figure. Once the figure is consecrated and it enters fully its role as stand-in for the otherworld mate, its owner in looking at the figure also looks at it in terms of cultural notions of beauty, its opposite sexual identity, its embodiment of youthful (or older) perfection, its personhood and gaze, as well as his or her own history and present lot. The crisis that led to its coming into being is always in the offing and it, too, frames the owner's experience of the image. The image is embedded within culturally and individually specific worldviews; it is there that it finds its meaning and creates the effects I have attempted to convey.

Outside this original context of creation and appreciation the *blolo* figure is no longer seen in the same way. What was an image is now only seen as form, its initial meaning has been lost, and new meanings have been imputed. The formal strength of the object, its sculptural volume, its stylized realism, and other artistic attributes are discerned by the outside eye and appreciated by other notions of aesthetics or intrigue. For most of this century, Baule figures were referred to as ancestor figures, yet they were discussed, displayed, and appreciated as art in spite of this misnomer.[1] The label was of little import; the figures were seen and appreciated as form, and the form itself was seen as the meaning. So, too, has been the reading of the form of the modern Baule figure interpreted as *colon*. The form has intrigued, even if it has been misread and misinterpreted.

The modern *colon* replica genre (that is, workshop-produced figures in clothed colonial style) was born from a perception of form in isolation. The *colon* became its own genre, living up to the newly invented meaning by becoming more and more responsive to the narrative invented around it. The meaning of the individual *colon,* nonetheless, lies in its typicality. No matter how accomplished and interesting, it is ultimately, I am convinced, mere illustration of an invented story.

The words of this volume, I trust, are words of imagination and empathy for the Baule *blolo* figure in its context of being. The figure for me, too, has been a vehicle of reverie that provides an aperture through which another world can be glimpsed and imagined—a world of art and meaning.

NOTES

PREFACE

1. See Ravenhill (1976 and 1978).

2. See Ravenhill (1988) for an introduction to the Goli among the Wan of central Côte d'Ivoire. I plan further publications on the Goli because of its never-ending complexities and reverberations in Wan social life.

3. Albert later assisted me and performed in a film on Baule figurative art that in part re-created his own experience: *Les Amants de l'au-delà: La Statuaire baoulé* (1982).

4. Some ideas in that paper have also been developed and expanded upon in my essay *The Self and the Other: Personhood and Images among the Baule of the Côte d'Ivoire* (1994), which explores the reasons that, of all the spirits recognized by the Baule, only two types are given human form.

CHAPTER 1. THE MEANING OF BAULE STATUES

1. See Vogel (1973; 1977: chap. 6) for a general discussion of Baule figure sculpture. The literal translation of *asie usu* is "earth-spirit," but since it functions as a generic term in the taxonomy of spirits, I shall use the term "nature spirit."

2. I have argued elsewhere (1994) that Baule figures described as *waka sran* are depicted as humans because of their "personhood." *Bo usu* seem to be considered more like fetishes (*amuin*) than spiritual agents with full personhood and volition; this may be one reason their forms are only minimally sculpted. They may be more "beings" than human.

3. The Baule word *amuin* is most often translated into French by the word *fétiche*, which has approximately the same sense as the English "fetish." For the Baule, the essential idea of "fetish" is a spiritual agency whose power can be applied or controlled by appropriate sacrifices (Ravenhill 1994).

4. On locational nouns see Timyan (1977:92–105).

5. It would appear that each person also has an otherworld father (*blolo si*), although the Baule discuss them less often than they do otherworld mothers, perhaps because they invoke the latter above all as explanatory agents of infant death.

6. Another, more common, solution revealed in divination may be to erect a small mound (*lo fannin*) of clay, kaolin, and leaves surmounted by a cowrie shell.

There is a feeling that this white clay stand-in is more "cooling" than a carved figure, which may well be more difficult to live with.

7. Étienne terminates this footnote by saying that "this is one more reason to consider that in Baule society masculine jealousy is strongly repressed."

8. My observations appear to be confirmed by Étienne's statement that "the *blolo bla* is rarely the object of a cult" (1966:368). Furthermore, it may well be the preponderance of male statues that has given rise to the erroneous notion that Baule statues are "ancestor figures." See Vogel (1973:23), who states that her observations in the field contradict "the widely held assumption that Baule figures were ancestor portraits."

Susan Vogel has pointed out to me that my sample probably also contained *asie usu* figures, although using the criteria she advances (1978:168) concerning the different surfaces of statues representing nature spirits and spirit-lovers, I would maintain that virtually all that I saw had the smooth patination associated with statues of spirit-lovers. For our understanding of Baule ideas concerning male and female roles it would be interesting to know whether *asie usu* are represented more often as male or as female.

9. B. Fride (1964:184) states that during his research in the early 1960s the average number of wives per married man was 1.24 among the Baule.

10. This is not to say, of course, that a woman only finds another man after she is divorced. It is often said that "a woman is like a cluster of palm nuts: when she falls, she takes the leaves with her" (*bla ti ke ae betre, s'e to o fa nnya*); that is, when a woman "falls" from her husband, she "lands" with another.

11. In general, one asks pardon either to excuse oneself or to demand a favor; the one asking pardon temporarily assumes an inferior position in order to receive dispensation.

12. The prefix *a-* is a nominalizing agent that changes the verb *to,* "to fall," into the substantive "fall." According to Olsen (1977), *nvle* has the sense of "change, augmentation, enlarging of affairs or goods" and gives rise to the greeting *nvleo,* which is given to one who has been away and has supposedly had a change in his situation.

The *atonvle* ceremony that effects the pardon of otherworld men occurs among the Saa and Warebo subgroups of the Baule, although Vogel (1978:157) states that it does not occur among the Akwe.

13. Again it would appear that the term *yasua* is used to designate a male with whom sexual relations are impossible.

14. *Ngoinman* is the most common form of divination among the Baule. An *ngoinman* diviner, almost always a man, manipulates nine leather thongs on each of which is knotted an object symbolizing social actors or physical and metaphysical concepts; the symbols represent: adult man, young man, adult woman, young woman, fire, earth, "thing," foot, and tooth. Jumbled together, and hidden by the diviner's hand, the thongs are drawn out and read in units of three. The symbols for young man, young woman, and fire, for example, could be read as adultery, depending always on what is being said by those who have asked for the consultation.

When the diviner uses a mouse oracle, the mouse, in eating, rearranges the positions of small beaded or bone shafts. The new arrangement of these elements is read by the diviner and interpreted, like the *ngoinman,* according to the dialogue with the client (Ravenhill 1994:24).

15. For more information on Baule aesthetics, see Vogel (1980), which was published simultaneously with my earlier essay (Ravenhill 1980), from which this section is derived.

16. Literally this should be translated as "neck lines," but since such lines are inherently beautiful, I prefer the gloss "beauty lines."

17. This is similar to the idea that black gums complement an already beautiful face and smile.

18. In relation to food and drink *yo fe* can be glossed as "tastes good"; there may thus be a play on the verb "eat," *di,* which also serves as a euphemism for sexual relations.

19. *Nenglen* can be glossed as either "thin" or "thinness"; thus *bo nenglen* can be translated as the "thinness of the base" or the "thinnest part of the *bo.*"

20. See Bell (1976:51) on fashion's interpretation of the bosom as a united mass or as separable breasts.

CHAPTER 2. THE EFFECT OF FASHION OF FORM

1. See, however, the discussion in chap. 5 on the replica genre of the *colon.*

2. A popular West African recording in the 1970s was *Petit N'imprudent,* which describes the actions and speech of an *ancien combattant* who is moved to anger by the actions of a neighbor's disrespectful child (Retord 1977). *Ancien combattants* also included veterans of the French army in World War I and in the war in Indochina.

3. In Baule society, relative age is one of the most important social distinctions; as a general rule one's social importance increases in direct proportion to one's age.

4. Compare the following forms: *waka ti* (tree top), *waka afien* (tree trunk/middle), and *waka bo* (tree base).

5. The Baule have borrowed the word for "waist" from the French *taille,* adapting it to Baule consonant and vowel patterns as *tayi.*

6. See also Martin and Koda (1994).

7. Scarification among the Baule was undertaken for individual aesthetic reasons rather than ethnic identification. Some scarification, however, may result from the application of medicine used to augment one's spiritual powers.

8. See Ortner (1974) and Ravenhill (1978) for discussions of woman as closer to nature than man.

9. See Weiskel (1980:214–15) on slaves and women as collaborators in the early colonial period.

CHAPTER 3. DREAMS, REVERIE, AND INDIVIDUAL EXISTENCE

1. See Ravenhill (1988) on the Goli masquerade.

2. It has been pointed out to me that his words could have been a simple monetary ploy, but I do not believe that this was his intent. He spoke so matter of factly that he brought into play a radically different reality, the *blolo.*

3. See Ravenhill (1994) on Baule notions of personhood in relation to *waka sran.*

CHAPTER 4. SEXUALITY, DESIRE AND VERSIMILITUDE

1. In my essay *The Self and the Other: Personhood and Images among the Baule of Côte d'Ivoire* (1994), I have attempted, following Étienne (1976), to give an overview of Baule ideas of culture, nature, and the supernatural. The essay focuses on the fundamental question of why two categories of supernatural spirits are represented materially, in art, as *persons,* that is, each as a person in wood (*waka sran*). In that essay I also develop certain ideas about the nature of a different type of supernatural spirit, or agent, called *amuin,* glossed as "fetish," that is a category of spirit having a supernatural force and powers that "can be usefully channelled when given a material support. . . . [I]t is the 'thingness' of the *amuin* that predominates. It is because the 'fetish' is a 'thing' that it can be appropriated, acquired, transported and used; it is a proprietary power" (p. 22).

Against this background of the general Baule understanding of *amuin,* how does one begin to understand the Baule idea that the Baule woman "possesses the greatest fetish that exists in Baule country: her sexual organs" (Guerry 1972:45)? I am now inclined to think that the answer lies in blood, specifically her menstrual blood. It is difficult to deal with the idea of the fetish given the historical baggage associated with the idea following both Freud and Marx, but my point in any case is not to deal with it at a universal level, only to elucidate Baule notions of the fetish.

The Baule say that it is "with blood that fetishes are made," and therein, I would argue, lies an understanding of Baule ideas about women and fetishes. The spilling of blood, and the taking of life, are male prerogatives among the Baule. Virtually all *amuin* are controlled by men because of their ongoing need of blood sacrifice. The *amuin,* despite its "natural" power, is at the same time a created thing, something dependent on man. It is something that is "captured." It is something that is obligated to react if the appropriate sacrifices are made. It is effective, yet somehow insufficient, for other fetishes will be needed. It is something that is external, a thing "out there."

Contrast the above notions to the Baule belief that the female sex organ, too, is a fetish. Now one has to deal with an entity that has different attributes. It is not created; it is a natural, primordial given, inherent rather than dependent. It is not captured; it inheres within. It acts, rather than reacts, and *then* demands the proper (blood) sacrifice. It is not insufficient; it is unique—the woman requires no other fetish. It is internal, not external. It is a thing within the female—an inextricable mix of "thingness" and personhood.

Suddenly, one begins to see that this particular *amuin,* the female sex, has a more independent, fundamentally different ontological status. It is, in a sense, a self-generating given. Blood, the generative element of the *amuin,* is inherent; the power of the female genitals is congenital. The female is thus the ultimate ambiguity: she is "person" and "thing" at the same time. Hence the power of her womanness. Perhaps this is why "the wife possesses the greatest fetish of all in Baule country: her sex" (Guerry 1972:45).

2. Many Baule figures found in museum or private collections have lost the *cache-sexe,* although patterns of wear may still indicate the exact areas of the hips, buttocks, and groin formerly covered.

3. One thinks of comparisons with the Luakina ceremony in Hawaii, in which the temple is sanctified when women wrap the god figures with cloth (Weiner 1992:86).

4. See Ravenhill (1994) on the personhood of *waka sran.*

5. In the past this activity was also undertaken to strengthen women's menfolk when they were off waging war (Delafosse 1913).

6. I follow Baxandall in calling the one who commissions the work of art his client rather than his patron. "The man who asked for, and found, a use for the painting might be called a *patron,* except this is a term that carries many overtones from other and different situations. The second party is an active, determining and not necessarily benevolent agent in the transaction of which the painting is a result: we can fairly call him a *client.*" (1972:1)

7. See Ravenhill (1994) for an overview of the ideas and methods of divination among the Baule.

8. "[R]everie is an oneiric activity in which a glimmer of consciousness subsists. The dreamer of reverie is present in his reverie" (Bachelard 1971:150).

9. It was more than twenty years ago, on the recommendation of Professor Tom Beidelman, that I first read Michael Baxandall's *Painting and Experience in Fifteenth-Century Italy* (1972) and his discussion of the "period eye." It was Baxandall's success in interpreting paintings as "the deposit of a social relationship" (p. 1) and his elucidation of the institutions and conventions in which quattrocento paintings were produced and appreciated that first inspired me to think that the cross-cultural interpretation of art might be possible.

10. An overview of Baule art is to be found in Ravenhill (in press).

11. See Vogel (1980:16) on her notion of "balanced asymmetry" as a "widespread feature of Baule style appreciated by the critics and consciously produced by the artists, although it is not a stated ideal."

12. See Vogel (1980:4–8) for a most insightful discussion of figurative and human resemblance. She notes that "[i]n commenting on the figures they were asked to rank, the Baule never used the particular 'it resembles a woman' or 'it resembles a man,' but always the generic *sran.*" I have discussed this sentence in Ravenhill (1994:35).

CHAPTER 5. OUTSIDE IMAGININGS

1. A full account of this period is to be found in Weiskel (1980).

2. For the French there was little ambiguity about the status of the *chef de canton.* In his discussion of the *chef de canton* as a colonial creation, F. J. Amon d'Aby cites an unpublished report (December 5, 1930) by the colonial administrator Maret arguing that the *chef de canton* "is not the continuator of the former indigenous petty king, who in times past exercised his authority on the basis of custom or violence, which we came to limit, moderate or control. Even when it is the same person, there is nothing in common between the former state of affairs and the present. The *chef de canton,* even if he is the descendant of a king with whom we had treatied, has no power unto himself. Named by us, by a choice in theory discretionary, he is, and he

is only our auxiliary. He places at our service his knowledge of the country, his influence, his prestige, and that is it. He only executes our orders. . . . It is the case of a level of administration that we created and that we impose, not a customary institution that we have maintained" (ca. 1988:30; my translation)

3. Jean-Pierre Chauveau and Jean-Pierre Dozon's provocative analysis of the economic and ethnic history of Côte d'Ivoire (1988) makes a major contribution to the analysis of Ivorian national history. It avoids dualistic frames of reference—*indigenes* versus *colons,* center versus periphery—and shows the ambiguities of the new colonial order in which local populations were often themselves the ones precipitating changes that the colonial government was hard put to deal with.

4. An idea of the ambience and ambiguities of this early period of French colonial power in Africa is found in the brilliant and powerfully evocative novel *L'Étrange destin du Wangrin* (1973) by Amadou Hampaté Ba, which portrays the life of a profiteering colonial interpreter and middleman in the French Soudan (now Mali), north of Côte d'Ivoire.

5. I use the French word *colon* as it has been used in the West African art market to indicate a figurative carving that depicts any type of modern clothing or headgear. The category thus includes Baule figures carved for Baule patrons as well as replica works of art intended for sale to foreign clients.

6. Wéréwéré Liking in her confusing book *Statues colons* (1987:10–11) argues that "not every painted statuette is necessarily a *colon,*" but she admits in effect that for African dealers there is often no opposition between the two.

7. I use quotation marks on the word "traditional" as a reminder of its conceptual ambiguity. It refers more to questions of presumed style than actual age (see also the discussion, in this chapter, of modern unclothed female figures being labeled "traditional").

8. The use of ethnic names as type categories for works of art is related to the whole history of the creation of ethnic identities in the Côte d'Ivoire that is critically discussed in Chauveau and Dozon (1988).

9. *Dyula* is not so much an ethnic ascription as a term for an "African trader, most often itinerant, (*no matter what his origin*) who buys and sells diverse forms of merchandise" (Équipe IFA 1988:120; emphasis added; my translation). In West African French, *dioula* sometimes overlaps with *haoussa:* "Muslim petty-trader, ambulant or having an inventory" (p. 178). Christopher Steiner (1991), on the Ivorian art market, uses these terms as though they referred to some real ethnic attributes; they do little but add an ethnological patina to the subject of study.

10. This type of tourist art and its production in the early seventies have been studied by Delores Richter (1980) among the Senufo professional carvers of the town of Korhogo.

11. Although my discussion is limited to the *colon* in terms of Baule art, I am convinced that other African visual traditions that began to incorporate aspects of modern fashion were misread in the same way. This has led to the grouping of many different works of art, from different cultural contexts and created with different intentionalities, as typical of the pan-African *colon* genre.

12. Steiner (1994:11–12) rightfully points out the feedback effect of commercial

publicity, such as Liking's book (1987) on market demand. Clémentine Deliss (1991:15) refers to Jahn's book *Colon* (1983) as now serving as a guideline for the art market in Africa.

13. This same position is found depicted on two Luba headrests, one in the British Museum and one in the National Museum of African Art, that were collected in Africa circa 1875.

14. I am following a fairly orthodox view of authenticity as it relates to African art, one advanced by a number of authors in the special issue of *African Arts* (1976) devoted to fakery and authenticity.

CHAPTER 6. VEHICLES OF REVERIE

1. Vogel's article "People of Wood: Baule Figure Sculpture" (1973) was the first correction of this misappellation.

BIBLIOGRAPHY

African Arts. 1976. Vol. 9, no. 3. Special issue: "Fakes, Fakers, and Fakery: Authenticity in African Art."

Les Amants de l'au-delà: La Statuaire baoulé. 1982. A film directed by Stéphan Kurc and produced by Les Films du Sabre for the French television channel TF1.

Amon d'Aby, F. J. ca. 1988. *Le problème des chefferies traditionnelles en Côte d'Ivoire.* Abidjan, Côte d'Ivoire: Nouvelles Editions Africaines.

Ashton, Dore, ed. 1985. *Twentieth-Century Artists on Art.* New York: Pantheon Books.

Ba, Amadou Hampaté. 1973. *L'Étrange destin du Wangrin.* Paris: Union Générale d'Éditions.

Bachelard, Gaston. 1971. *The Poetics of Reverie: Childhood, Language, and the Cosmos.* Boston: Beacon Press.

Bateson, Gregory. 1973. "Style, Grace, and Information in Primitive Art." In *Primitive Art and Society,* edited by Anthony Forge. London: Oxford University Press, for the Wenner-Gren Foundation for Anthropological Research.

Baxandall, Michael. 1972. *Painting and Experience in Fifteenth-Century Italy.* London: Oxford University Press.

Bell, Quentin. 1976. *On Human Finery.* London: Hogarth Press.

Benjamin, Andrew. 1991. *Art, Mimesis, and the Avant-Garde: Aspects of a Philosophy of Difference.* London: Routledge.

Berger, John. 1972. *Ways of Seeing.* London: BBC and Penguin.

Binoche et Godeau. 1987. *"Série Noire": Art colon et style tribal—vente du dimanche 8 mars 1987 à 14 heures.* Paris.

———1990. *"Colons"—vente du mercredi 6 juin 1990 à 14 heures 15.* Paris.

Brenson, Michael. 1992. "Quality and Other Things." *American Art* 6, no. 4:2–16.

Carteron, Michel. 1972. *Petit lexique baoulé-français.* Bocanda, Côte d'Ivoire: Mission Catholique. Mimeographed.

Chauveau, Jean-Pierre, and Jean-Pierre Dozon. 1988. "Ethnies et état en Côte d'Ivoire." In *L'Anthropologie politique d'aujourd'hui,* edited by Michel Izard. Special issue of *Revue française de science politique* 38, no. 5:732–47.

Crowder, Michael. 1971. *West African Resistance: The Response to Colonial Occupation.* London: Hutchinson.

Crownover, David. 1960. "The Pink People." *Expedition* 2, no. 3:33–35.

Delafosse, Maurice. 1913. "Coutumes observées par les femmes en temps de guerre chez les Agni de la Côte d'Ivoire." *Revue d'ethnographie de de sociologie* 4:226–68.

Deliss, Clémentine. 1991. "Cultures . . . Objects . . . Identities." In *Exotic Europeans*. London: South Bank Centre.

den Tuinder, Bastiaan A. 1978. *Ivory Coast: The Challenge of Success*. Baltimore: Johns Hopkins University Press.

Dutton, Dennis. 1977. "Art, Behavior, and the Anthropologists." *Current Anthropology* 18, no. 3:387–407.

Duvignaud, Jean. 1972. *The Sociology of Art*. New York: Harper and Row.

Effimbra, Georges. 1959. *Manuel de baoulé*. Paris: Fernand Nathan.

Équipe IFA. 1983. *Inventaire des particularités lexicales du Français en Afrique Noire*. Paris: AUPELF.

Eschenberg, Myron. 1991. *Colonial Conscripts: The "Tirailleurs Sénégalais" in French West Africa, 1857–1960*. Portsmouth, N.H.: Heinemann.

Étienne, Pierre. 1964. "Essai d'analyse des interdictions de mariage baoulé." In *Étude régionale de Bouaké*. Abidjan, Côte d'Ivoire: Ministère du Plan.

———. 1966. "Phénomènes réligieux et facteurs socio-économiques dans un village baoulé de la région de Bouaké (Côte d'Ivoire)." *Cahiers d'Études africaines* 6, no. 3:367–401.

———. 1972. *Les Interdictions de mariage chez les baoulé*. Abidjan, Côte d'Ivoire: ORSTOM.

———. 1976. "Le fait villageois baoulé." *Communautés rurales et paysanneries tropicales*. Travaux et documents de l'ORSTOM, no. 53: 27–91.

Étienne, Pierre, and Mona Étienne. 1964. "L'Organisation sociale des baoulé." In *Les Populations communes de la Côte d'Ivoire et du Ghana*. Proceedings of the Colloque inter-universitaire Ghana-Côte d'Ivoire, Bondoukou, Côte d'Ivoire, January 1974.

———. 1971. "A qui mieux mieux ou le mariage chez les baoulé." *Cahiers ORSTOM: Série sciences humaines* 8, no. 2:165–86.

Focillon, Henri. 1992. *The Life of Forms in Art*. New York: Zone Books.

Freedberg, David. 1989. *The Power of Images: Studies in the History and Theory of Response*. Chicago: University of Chicago Press.

Fride, B. 1964. "L'Analyse démographique de la population actuelle." In *Étude régionale de Bouaké*. Abidjan, Côte d'Ivoire: Ministère du Plan.

Guerry, Vincent (R.P.). 1972. *La Vie quotidienne dans un village baoulé*. Abidjan, Côte d'Ivoire: INADES.

Hallpike, C. R. 1969. "Social Hair." *Man*, n.s., 4, no. 2: 256–64.

Hudson, Liam, and Bernadine Jacot. 1991. *The Way Men Think: Intellect, Intimacy, and the Erotic Imagination*. New Haven: Yale University Press.

Hunt, Harry T. 1989. *The Multiplicity of Dreams: Memory, Imagination, and Consciousness*. New Haven: Yale University Press.

Jahn, Jens. 1983. *Colon: Das schwarze Bild vom Weissen mann*. Munich: Rogner and Bernhard.

Leach, Edmund. 1961. "Time and False Noses." In *Rethinking Anthropology*. London: Athlone Press.

Lesser, Wendy. 1991. *His Other Half: Men Looking at Women through Art.* Cambridge: Harvard University Press.

Liking, Wéréwéré. 1987. *Statues colons: Statuettes peintes de l'Afrique de l'Ouest.* Abidjan, Côte d'Ivoire: NEA-Arhis.

Lips, Julius. 1937. *The Savage Hits Back.* New Haven: Yale University Press.

Lucie-Smith, Edward. 1991. *Sexuality in Western Art.* New York: Thames and Hudson.

MacCannell, Dean. 1989. *The Tourist: A New Theory of the Leisure Class.* New York: Shocken Books.

Martin, Richard, and Harold Koda. 1994. *Waist Not: The Migration of the Waist, 1800–1960.* New York: Metropolitan Museum of Art.

Olsen, Jean. 1977. "Baule-English Dictionary." Manuscript. Mission Protestante, Bouaké, Côte d'Ivoire.

Ortner, Sherry. 1974. "Is Female to Male as Nature Is to Culture?" In *Woman, Culture, and Society,* edited by Michelle Zimbalist Rosaldo and L. Lamphere. Stanford: Stanford University Press.

Pellizzi, Francesco. 1990–91. Editorial. *RES* 19–20:5–7.

Ravenhill, Philip L. 1976. *The Social Organization of the Wan: A Patrilineal People of Ivory Coast.* Ann Arbor, Mich.: University Microfilms.

———. 1978. "The Interpretation of Symbolism in Wan Female Initiation." *Africa* 48, no. 1:66–78.

———. 1980. *Baule Statuary Art: Meaning and Modernization.* Working Papers in the Traditional Arts, no. 5. Philadelphia: Institute for the Study of Human Issues.

———. 1981. "Le musée du prophète Djouman-Mihin, Vavoua, Côte d'Ivoire." *Godo-Godo.* Revue de l'Institut d'Histoire, d'Art, et d'Archéologie africains, no. 6: 128–43.

———. 1985. *Dans leur milieu: La statuaire baoulé, les autels lobi.* Abidjan, Côte d'Ivoire: CEDA and Les Publications du Ministère des Affaires Culturelles.

———. 1988. "An African Triptych: On the Interpretation of Three Parts and the Whole." *Art Journal* 47, no. 2:88–94.

———. 1993. *Dreaming the Other World: Figurative Art of the Baule, Côte d'Ivoire.* Washington, D.C.: National Museum of African Art.

———. 1994. *The Self and the Other: Personhood and Images among the Baule of Côte d'Ivoire.* Monograph Series, no. 28. Los Angeles: Fowler Museum of Cultural History.

———. In press. "Baule." *The Dictionary of Art.* London: Macmillan.

Ravenhill, Philip L., and Roslyn A. Walker. 1988. *Kalabari Ancestral Screens: Levels of Meaning.* Washington, D.C.: National Museum of African Art.

Read, Herbert. 1931. *The Meaning of Art.* Baltimore: Penguin Books.

Retord, Georges. 1977. "Petit N'imprudent." *Recherche, Pedagogie, et Culture* 5, no. 29–30:35–43

Richter, Delores. 1980. *Art, Economics, and Change: The Kulebele of Northern Ivory Coast.* La Jolla, Calif.: Psych/Graphic Publishers.

Roberts, Andrew, ed. 1990. *The Colonial Movement in Africa: Essays on the Movement of Minds and Materials, 1900–1940.* New York: Cambridge University Press.

Simic, Charles. 1992. *Dime-Store Alchemy: The Art of Joseph Cornell.* Hopewell, N.J.: Ecco Press.

Simmel, Georg. 1955. *"Conflict" and "The Web of Group Affiliations."* Translated by Kurt Wolff and Reinhard Bendix, respectively. New York: Free Press.

Solomon-Godeau, Abigail. 1993. "The Legs of the Countess." In *Fetishism as Cultural Discourse,* edited by Emily Apter and William Petz. Ithaca: Cornell University Press.

Steiner, Christopher. 1991. "The Trade in West African Art." *African Arts* 24, no. 1: 38–43, 100–101.

———. 1994. *African Art in Transit.* New York: Cambridge University Press.

Stewart, Susan. 1984. *On Longing: Narratives of the Miniature, the Gigantic, the Souvenir, the Collection.* Durham, N.C.: Duke University Press.

Timyan, Judith. 1977. "A Discourse-Based Grammar of Baule: The Kodè Dialect." Ph.D. diss., City University of New York.

Trubetzkoy, N. S. 1949. *Principes de phonologie.* Paris: Klincksieck.

Vogel, Susan Mullin. 1973. "People of Wood: Baule Figure Sculpture." *Art Journal* 33, no. 1:23–26.

———. 1978. *Baule Art as an Expression of a Worldview.* Ann Arbor, Mich.: University Microfilms.

———. 1980. *Beauty in the Eyes of the Baule: Aesthetics and Cultural Values.* Working Papers in the Traditional Arts, no. 6. Philadelphia: Institute for the Study of Human Issues.

Walton, Kendall L. 1990. *Mimesis as Make-Believe: On the Foundations of the Representational Arts.* Cambridge: Harvard University Press.

Weiner, Annette. 1992. *Inalienable Possessions: The Paradox of Keeping-While-Giving.* Berkeley and Los Angeles: University of California Press.

Weiskel, Timothy C. 1980. *French Colonial Rule and the Baule Peoples: Resistance and Collaboration, 1889–1911.* Oxford: Clarendon Press.